LD CHAMPIO
ISTONS

The Detroit Pistons
1989 - 90

by Roland Lazenby

Photographs by Kirthmon Dozier
of *The Detroit News*

TAYLOR PUBLISHING COMPANY
Dallas, Texas

Design by Karen Lazenby

©1989, Roland Lazenby
Taylor Publishing Company
1550 West Mockingbird Lane, Dallas, Texas 75235

Library of Congress Cataloging-in-Publication Data

Lazenby, Roland.
    The Detroit Pistons : 1989-90 / Roland Lazenby.
            p.   cm.
    ISBN 0-87833-678-8
    1. Detroit Pistons (Basketball team)   I. Title
GV885.52.D47L39   1989   89-5051
796.323 '64' 0977434--dc20   CIP

Printed in the United States of America

(Einstein photo)

Contents

The Daly Double?

It seems that every season needs a handle. For 1988-89, when the Los Angeles Lakers were hoping to win their third straight NBA title, coach Pat Riley came up with the notion of "Three-peat." In the modern spirit of get everything that you can while you can, Riley reportedly patented the term.

In retrospect, that wasn't such a bad idea. The Lakers didn't win the title, but Riley still won the lottery. Sporting goods stores and airport gift shops across the country spent the year hawking Three-peat shirts and bumper stickers.

Now that 1989-90 is upon us and the Pistons are defending World Champions, Coach Chuck Daly has tried to hold down all the talk about his team repeating. It just puts unnecessary pressure on the players, Daly explained.

At the same time, nobody knows better than Daly that every sword has a double edge. So, just in case, he's already come up with the handle for the Pistons' 1989-90 quest.

The Daly Double.

Not bad.

Not Bad Boys, either.

The Pistons, of course, have been the Bad Boys for the past two seasons. But heading into 1989-90, doubt surrounds that moniker for a few good reasons. First, power forward Rick Mahorn, the player who epitomized the Pistons' Badness, was lost to the Minnesota Timberwolves in last June's expansion draft, leading Isiah Thomas to declare that the term Bad Boys would be laid to rest. (But, in the Riley spirit, when Thomas released his book on the championship season in July, he called it "Bad Boys.")

The league is also said to take a dim view of the term. Yet it was NBA Properties that started all the trouble in the first place by creating and then marketing the 1988 video "Bad Boys."

Frankly, Chuck Daly doesn't know what will happen with Bad Boys. "I think it will be difficult to put aside," he said just before training camp opened. "I don't know if we'll want to."

The down side of the Bad Boys tag is the attention it draws from officials and the league, which resulted in fouls, fines and suspensions, Daly said.

And the positive side? "I think people now understand that it gave our club and our league more personality," Daly said. "Unfortunately, our front office never patented the term."

Still, it is on the court, not at the patent office, where the Pistons' hopes for a repeat must be registered. There should be plenty of continuity for 1989-90, and a few changes, the major one being the loss of Mahorn.

"His leadership was an abstract thing," Daly said of Mahorn. "He was a very physical, intimidating player. We're gonna miss those attributes."

Added as a backup to help fill the void was 6'9" Scott Hastings, a free agent who played last season with the Miami Heat and before that with Atlanta.

"He gives us a veteran player who has size and shooting ability," General Manager Jack McCloskey said. "On defense, he'll do an adequate job. He will more or less give us the depth we've had in the past. Plus a good individual to have on your team."

Daly agreed: "I think Scott is a very solid player, an excellent passer, a tough kid. I think he'll fit in. It'll be interesting to see."

The same could be said of Anthony Cook, the prime rookie in the Pistons camp. Detroit originally drafted Illinois small forward Kenny Battle as the 27th pick of the first round, but then traded him and backup guard Michael Williams to Phoenix for the 6'9" Cook, who had been taken as the 24th player in the first round.

Cook is a Pistons type player, having set the career Pac-10 shotblocking record at the University of Arizona. He also led the Wildcats in rebounding his last two seasons there and averaged better than 60 percent from the floor. The only liability seems to be his weight, 205, but he will have time to bulk up. In the interim, he should be a nice addition for those late-game workouts so typical of the Pistons bench.

As for the veterans, team leader Isiah Thomas is said to be recharged and ready to go to training camp. The same was true of Bill Laimbeer and the rest of the Bad Boys. Uh. The not-so Bad Boys? The Daly Doublers? Whatever you call 'em, the early reports say they're ready.

Even Mark Aguirre, who reportedly had ballooned above 250 pounds right after the championship, weighed in as slim and trim late in the summer. "I've heard that," Daly said of Aguirre's weight. "But that doesn't mean anything. He can put on 10 pounds in a day. I think he can go back to being a premier player in this league. I don't think he can do that and keep all the weight."

That's why the Pistons have their strong bench, Daly said. "And that's where Dennis Rodman's situation comes in. He's pushed everybody who has ever been in that starting forward position. That makes it competitive."

Rodman will see more minutes.

Daly wants to patent the NBA title.

Speaking of premier players, Daly said Rodman had elevated his game to that level. "He's one of the best sixth men in the league." With Mahorn's departure, Rodman is sure to play more minutes, but the coaching staff hasn't decided to make him a starter.

"I just like the fact that he comes off the bench," Daly said.

Among those fascinating questions for the Bad ones, the big one still stands out. Can they repeat? You won't know that until they get into the exhibition season and the schedule. "It's the most difficult schedule we've had here," Daly said, a comment he seems to make each season, yet also a comment that grows in truth each year. "We play 17 of our first 27 on the road. That's not all bad. It does give the club a challenge."

In past seasons, the Pistons have used the early road schedule to get a leg up on the league. I wouldn't bet against 'em in '90.

That's a wrap on the forecast. What lies ahead is the second edition of the Pistons yearbook. We hope you enjoy it.

Thanks go out to Arnie Hanson, the publisher at Taylor Publishing Company, for his continued belief in the project. The same goes for Matt Dobek, the Pistons

director of public relations. The photographic work of Kirthmon Dozier (*The Detroit News*) remains the redeeming feature. We also wish to thank photographic contributors Andy Bernstein of the NBA, Allen Einstein of the Pistons and Steve Lipofsky of the Boston Celtics.

The input of the Pistons public relations staff was vital. Special thanks to Debbie Mayfield and Dave Wieme. As for editors, I must thank Mike Nahrstedt of The Sporting News and Jim Donovan of Taylor Publishing. Additional editorial assistance was provided by Tim Orwig, Richard Lovegrove and Bob Hartman.

The Pistons players also deserve much credit for taking the time to answer questions and explain their views on the championship season.

Additional thanks go to *The Detroit News* and *Detroit Free Press*, two fine sports sections. The folks at *The Oakland Press* also do a great job.

The final tribute should go to Chuck Daly, who has already given us a handle on the upcoming season. Here's a toast to the Daly Double. Let's hope it has a nice Ring to it.

Roland Lazenby

Above: Dumars with his father, Joe Dumars II. Below: With his mom, Ophelia Dumars, at Joe Dumars Appreciation Day.

The Family Dumars, An American Classic

For Joe Dumars, the eye opener came 11 years ago, just days after he turned 15. It was the first morning of the summer of 1978, and the time had come for him to work on his father's truck route, just as his five older brothers before him had worked.

For nearly a quarter century, his father, Joe Dumars II, had followed the same grueling schedule, up at four each morning, back home each night by 10:30 or 11. Usually, in the earlier years, if it wasn't too late when he got home, Mr. Dumars would line his sons up and ask them about their day. With muscles thick across his chest and arms, he was the kind of father boys marvel at. Most nights he brought home some small joke or instructive rhyme to tell his children.

As might be expected, young Joe was excited about this first time on the truck with his father. So he was up early, about 3:30, and eager to get out on the road. Once his large bedroom had been filled with brothers, but they were all out on their own now, and Joe had the room to himself. His older sister, Martha, was gone, too, off to college, and the house was empty and quiet, save for his parents slumbering in their bedroom.

"I remember getting up," Dumars says, "putting my light on back in my room, getting dressed, and sitting there waiting to go. I flipped on my television with the sound down and sat on the edge of the bed waiting for him to get up."

Finally, he heard his father stirring.

With muscles thick across his chest and arms, he was the kind of father boys marvel at. Most nights he brought home some small joke or instructive rhyme to tell his children.

"He walked back," Dumars recalls, "looked in at me and asked, 'You ready already?' 'Yeah,' I told him, 'I'm ready.' "

It seemed to take forever for his father to get his coffee. Finally he came back to Joe's room. "Let's roll," he said.

Each morning in the darkness, his father left the Dumars' brick house in Natchitoches, a small town in north-central Louisiana, and drove 52 miles south to Alexandria, where he picked up an 18-wheeler loaded with 20,000 to 30,000 pounds of groceries. Over the course of the day, Mr. Dumars would drive across northwest Louisiana and eastern Texas, stopping to deliver groceries at dozens of stores along the way. Each day, he dispersed 10 to 15 tons of goods that way, one dolly load at a time.

Joe Dumars remembers heading back north that morning with his father and the day's load. Young Joe was riding high, bouncing along, full of expectations. The sun was coming

up, the miles were rolling by, and the aroma of his father's King Edward cigar filled the cab. If this was manhood and work and responsibility, then it wasn't bad at all, he remembers thinking.

Yet that morning, so plump with potential, was punctured directly. By the fourth or fifth stop and with all the unloading involved, rolling in dolly after dolly of boxed groceries, Joe Dumars quickly gained a new view of the working world. "I was worn out," Dumars says now. "I remember thinking, 'How has he been doing this all these years?' "

They had yet to reach lunchtime of Joe's first day on the job.

There was one other thing that impressed Joe from that first look at his father's typical day. At every stop, Mr. Dumars was welcomed. "The people in the stores were happy to see my father," Dumars says. "Some of them had things for him to eat. It was obvious people liked him."

Now 63 and retired, Mr. Dumars smiles at his son's recounting of that day. "It was a job, I'll tell you that," he says. "I was fortunate enough to take all my sons out there with me and learn them how to work. I think that helped shape their lives. Out of the six, every one of them, they don't mind tackling work."

The Detroit Pistons have firsthand knowledge of only one of Mr. Dumars' sons, that being Joe III. But they can confirm that the youngest lives up to his father's standards. Every night.

In fact, the testimonials to Mr. Dumars' son come so fast and furious

Dumars dishes off against Seattle.

these days they've almost become a litany. Joe Dumars has no ego. Joe Dumars sacrifices his scoring for the team. Joe Dumars could be an All-Star if he weren't so unselfish. Joe Dumars is a great defensive player. Joe Dumars is the ultimate professional. Joe Dumars does the job quietly. Joe Dumars epitomizes class. Joe Dumars is just another Joe. Like Dumars' reputation, this litany has grown quietly and steadily since he entered the league four seasons ago as the 18th pick in the first-round of the 1985 NBA draft.

The praise reached a crescendo of sorts this past spring when the 26-year-old Dumars was named Most Valuable Player of the 1989 NBA Finals. He earned that honor by leading the Pistons to the first league championship in their history, won with a 4-0 sweep of the Los Angeles Lakers in the Finals. He was the team's top scorer against the Lakers, averaging 27.3 points per game. A month later, the Pistons rewarded this effort with a new, six-year $8 million contract that more than doubled his 1988-89 salary.

"He deserves it," Pistons General Manager Jack McCloskey said. "I think he's certainly in the upper echelon of guards in the league. His value is on both ends of the court, and he's demonstrated that for years. And there's his attitude. There are very few players in the league, and very few people in any facet of business, with the good outlook, the wholesome outlook, that Joe has."

Prior to last season's playoffs, the 6'3" guard was considered one of the best-kept secrets in basketball, primarily because he played in the shadow of Isiah Thomas, the Pistons colorful point guard. But in the aftermath of the championship, Dumars was swept away in a tide of celebrity. Normally a controlled, measured kind of guy, he obviously struggled to keep his emotions in check amid the din of celebration in the Pistons locker room.

The Pistons, as you probably know, were the Bad Boys, and Joe Dumars was their resident Good Guy. The Bad Boys gave hard fouls, woofed a lot and grinned somewhat nasty, somewhat insane grins. Dumars played quiet and steady defense, provided outbursts of scoring when necessary and otherwise blended into the background. On a roster bristling with personalities, Dumars seemed inordinately plain.

"I can understand," he says, "that people want to see the fancy stuff. But, believe me, we've got enough fancy stuff on the Detroit Pistons where I don't have to be fancy."

As for the Bad Boys image, Dumars says he enjoyed it: "I just don't get wrapped up into being one of the Bad Boys. I like it though, I really do."

In seeking a way to maintain his calm among the characters on the team, Dumars says he looked to his father. "I compare myself here to the way he was on his job," he explains. "I think everyone liked him. A lot of truckers are some rough guys. For him at his work, it was almost like it is here for me, he was one of the good guys with the bad guys, the Bad Boys. Because those truckers are some bad boys. He was one of the good guys. He drove the speed limit and didn't hog the road."

Like his dad, Dumars goes the limit and never hogs the lane. Even the jubilation of the championship did little to alter his modus operandi. After claiming their shiny trophy, his teammates were a rowdy bunch of pirates, hoisting their skulls and crossbones, spewing champagne, chanting "Bad Boys" over and over and doing lots of hearty horse laughs, while Dumars quietly retreated to the back of the locker room to answer a few questions.

His answers were as steady and colorless as his play. How did it feel to win the MVP? some guy with a mike asked.

"Great," Dumars said. "Absolutely great."

"Hey Joe," somebody interrupted. "CBS wants you, Joe. CBS wants you."

Before he could acknowledge the network's request for an on-camera interview, teammate Vinnie Johnson

... and penetrates against Chicago.

The challenge, he said in an aside during the locker room victory celebration, is to keep your emotions from blasting through the ceiling, and going skyward, taking your ego with them.

yelled from across the room. "Broadway Joe! Yo, yo, yo."

Broadway Joe? Dumars says he wants to be recognized for his ability, yet when the media comes in waves like this, he meets the onslaught with a fluttering smile and retreats a little further into the background.

The challenge, he said in an aside during the locker room victory celebration, is to keep your emotions from blasting through the ceiling, and going skyward, taking your ego with them.

Actually, Joe Dumars would have preferred to be at home with his family at that instant. "Not that I don't want to be here with these people," he said as he watched teammate Mark Aguirre hug Vinnie Johnson. But it was a matter of time and space. If someone could just park a time machine outside the locker room so that he could beam himself down home to Louisiana...

The next best thing to being there, of course, is the telephone. Dumars is not a man of many indulgences. But Ma Bell is one of them. Every night after every game, Joe Dumars hustles out of the locker room to phone home. The championship night was no different. After four years in the pros, he had the routine down. First he dialed his mom. Then his fiancee, Debbie Nelson, who became his wife in September. Then his best friend from college, John Wesley.

When he feels the craziness of the NBA pulling him out of reality, these are the people who hold Joe Dumars down to earth.

Dumars spent his effort in the Chicago series trying to contain Jordan.

He saved his best effort for the Lakers.

BOOPIE

All this praise is well and good, says his mother, Ophelia Dumars, but if the truth be known, little Joe—known as "Boopie" to the family—was quite spoiled as a child. The problem, she says, is that Joe, the youngest of the seven children, and Martha, the third youngest and the only girl in the group, vied for her attention.

"If I would do something with her," Mrs. Dumars says, "he'd get mad. I had to separate those two because they were always jealous of each other. It got to be a problem, until I got them both together and told them they were special."

Joe Dumars smiles when told of his mother's recollection. "Yeah," he says. "I remember that. I remember being spoiled, wanting to get my way, and I would fight to get my way. I remember her talking to me. She explained to me that I was special and that I didn't have anything to worry about, that I had a place in the home.

"Sometimes you get the feeling, with so many other kids around, that they are giving one or two more attention on that particular day. You may feel that they are more special than you."

It has always been important to Joe Dumars, in his own quiet way, to know that he is special.

Joe is special, says his father. "I'm very proud of Joe for all his accomplishments, but like I say to everyone, 'I've got five more boys and all of them make me proud.' They've all turned out to be nice and respectful young men. I understand Joe's position. It's great to make it to the NBA. Thousands of children would like to make it that far. But as for my other sons, if they're making a living and being honorable, that makes me just as proud as the one that's in the limelight."

As their father says, the Dumars offspring are a special group. Ronald, 35, is a truck driver like his father.

Paul, the next youngest, is an accountant with the city of Shreveport.

David, who played for the Denver Gold of the United States Football League, now works as an assistant football coach at Southeast Missouri State.

Danny is the assistant manager of the Greyhound terminal in Natchitoches. And Martha is a dietitian living in New York.

But perhaps the most special Dumars of all is Mark, two years older than Joe. He lives in Natchitoches and works as an orderly in a nursing home. You could be asked to list 100 probable professions for the brother of an NBA star, and nursing home orderly wouldn't be among them. Yet if you've ever had a loved one in long-term care, you already know that caring, sensitive orderlies are the people who make trying conditions seem bearable. In their quiet way, orderlies often do more real doctoring than the doctors themselves.

Of all his siblings, Joe is closest to Mark. "That's his special brother," Ophelia Dumars explains. "Little kids, older people, they all just love him." Mark has a special feeling for those older patients at the home without families. During holidays, he takes them candy and fruit, and spends time with them on his weekends off, his mother says.

"He's the most sensitive, caring person I know," Joe says.

Again, that doesn't mean the two

Dumars has come into his own as an offensive performer.

brothers haven't had their times. Being the two youngest boys in the family, they played and competed continuously at every game available. "You could always tell when Mark beat him," Mr. Dumars says with a laugh. "Joe would start to cry and fight. Mark would outdo him, and you could tell because there would be a fight."

Being the baby of the family made Joe stronger, Mark says in his brother's defense. "He played all the time with older kids, some of them six to seven years older. He would get hit and knocked down and start crying."

Being the youngest had another drawback in that eventually Joe was the only child. Ophelia Dumars recalls that late summer afternoon that her older children all loaded in the car and headed off to college. "Joe was standing in the doorway with me, waving goodbye," she says, "and he turned to me and said, 'I want to go, too.' When Mark went off to college that really hurt him. Joe had never worried about having other kids as friends because his brothers and sister were his buddies."

Basketball had become his companion before Mark left, but the relationship with the game became even more intense afterward. "It was something you could do alone," Dumars explained. "You didn't always have to get up a group of people."

Across the street from the Dumars home is the largest liquor store in Natchitoches. It had giant floodlights that used to shine on the Dumars' back yard, illuminating the goal Mr. Dumars had built for his sons. There, Mrs. Dumars says, Joe would often shoot alone until late at night when his father came home.

Certainly Joe Dumars epitomizes the team aspects of basketball, yet that solitary essence remains very much a part of his game.

THE CHOICE

Ask Dumars his fondest memories of childhood and he has a ready answer: "Playing pickup games," he says. "Either football, baseball or basketball. Playing those game out in the field. Playing all the time. Having great games, competing

Isiah and Joe enjoyed the championship parade.

Dumars scored 42 against Cleveland as Detroit clinched the regular season title.

Mr. Dumars did the unthinkable in Louisiana. He suggested his son drop football and play basketball exclusively. At the end of the season, Dumars did just that.

against other little boys. I'll always remember that."

Those games were even better than what he faces in the NBA, he says, "because, after a while here it becomes a grind almost. It becomes just routine. With those games there was so much anticipation, being in school thinking, 'After school today we are going to play against those guys. They might have beat us yesterday, but we are going to beat them today.' So those games, they were really special. This becomes a business almost, you have your accountants, you have your attorneys, you have all that. With that it was strictly that game and that's all that mattered.

"I loved those games," he says. "There is nothing at stake but talking about it. But that's a lot. That's the way it was. That's all we had were those games, and they meant the world to us at the time."

In the hill-country culture of northwest Louisiana, the preferred sport is football. All five of Joe's older brothers played before him. Joe followed right in their footsteps. As a ninth grader, he started at tailback on an undefeated junior high team. But he took a beating that year, and with each hit he decided he liked football less. One day a larger player rang his bell in practice, and Joe expressed his displeasure when his father got home that night.

Mr. Dumars did the unthinkable in Louisiana. He suggested his son drop football and play basketball exclusively. At the end of the season, Dumars did just that. His decision brought an outcry from the adults and even school administrators in the

When it came to trophy time, Dumars was subdued.

overdo it. I told his mother about it and asked her to stop it. She asked him not to play at night, but Joe would always slip out of the house and wind up over at the gym again." Young players with that kind of drive are usually headed somewhere, Garrett says.

As a 6'2" sophomore, Dumars started at forward on the junior varsity, although he performed many of the ballhandling chores. Most of the players on the team were only about six feet, but by his junior year, Dumars started at guard on the varsity.

"Even then Joe had a shooting range of 20 to 23 feet," Garrett says. "And he had unshakeable confidence in his shot." The team played a lot of pressure, man-to-man defense, Garrett says. "We just got right at people. Joe loved the defense."

Just as his junior season started, Dumars, then 16, took an evening job at a Church's Fried Chicken store managed by his cousin. Each day after practice he'd head to work, where he faced a multiplicity of tasks: cutting raw chickens into pieces on a meat saw; frying the parts; working the cash register, cleaning, whatever needed to be done. As Dumars explains it, on another job he might have been able to let things slide a bit, but this was his cousin's store, and you couldn't let a cousin down.

"I look back on it and it was good experience," he says. "Even at the time, though, I liked it. Most of the time it was me and somebody else there and I liked always being in charge. Even though I wasn't running the whole thing it was like I had a lot of responsibility there. I feel, give me some responsibility and I'll show you I can get it done. I like that."

That "get-it-done" mentality evidenced itself in Dumars' game as well. He wanted the ball in key situations. His senior season, 1980-81, his team challenged for the district championship. In a tight late-season game against Captain Shreve High School, the scored was tied with minutes left. Dumars was in a scoring trance. "We called a time out," Garrett says. "Joe told me in the huddle,

community. "That boy's making a terrible mistake," Dumars recalls them saying.

J.D. Garrett is something of a utility man in Natchitoches, coaching track, football and basketball . A star running back at Grambling who later played for the New England Patriots, Garrett's first love was football, but he made no attempt to dissuade Dumars from his decision. It was obvious,

Garrett says, "Joe loved basketball better."

Dumars would practice basketball with the junior varsity team for two to three hours each day after school, go home for dinner, then head to the gym at nearby Northwestern Louisiana to run the floor with the college boys. "He wouldn't get home until 10 or 11 at night," Garrett says. "I was concerned because a kid can

'Give me the ball, Coach, and I'll get you that district championship.' "

His jumper was almost unstoppable. "Like a layup," Garrett said, "and we got the championship." That scenario has repeated itself at key times for the Pistons. They won the hotly contested Central Division championship in Cleveland when Dumars scored 42 points with 11 assists and no turnovers. His scoring surges did a similar job

against the Lakers in the championship series. Yet Dumars accomplishes these runs without customary wildness. "He always played under control," Garrett says. "Nobody worried him. He never let them."

One day in practice, Garrett told Dumars that he had the ability to play professional basketball. It was a big statement for a high school coach to make, but Dumars remembers it as a major block in the foundation of his confidence.

Although he wasn't overwhelmed by colleges, Dumars began to receive some attention from recruiters during his senior year. And his parents suggested that perhaps he should quit the job at Church's, because cutting chickens on high-powered saws didn't seem like such a good idea for someone who had a chance to earn an athletic scholarship.

The primary suitors were Mississippi State, Louisiana Tech, Northwestern Louisiana, and McNeese State. Dale Brown from LSU made a brief appearance at one of Dumars' games, but the gym was packed and Brown left after staying a few minutes, Garrett recalls.

At first, Dumars leaned toward Mississippi State, but a coaching turnover there changed his mind. Louisiana Tech and Northwestern both ran tightly controlled offenses, so Dumars chose McNeese, which ran an up-tempo offense, where his shooting could be a factor. McNeese, a small liberal arts school in Lake Charles, Louisiana, sat in the midst of the Cajun country.

As a player, his impact was

In his first four years in the league, Dumars became known for his defense.

immediate. John Wesley, who came to the team in the same recruiting class, recalls Dumars was obviously unique. "He was so mature," Wesley says. "He always took on so much responsibility. He came in as a freshman and had to lead us, the entire team, including the older players."

"It was a great experience for me," Dumars says, "because I really had to learn responsibility, I mean really. Because, I had to carry a big load, but I enjoyed it. I enjoyed having to carry the load. I enjoyed having to be the one to set the example. And I led by example.

"I never said much, but I just worked hard everyday. And I never tried—as the star—to get away with more than the other guys did, which happens a lot of the times. You know, maybe slough off a little bit and not do as much as the other guys do. I worked just as hard so everybody else had to work hard."

At McNeese, however, a pattern developed where the coaches increasingly relied on Dumars. He became known as a scorer, but while he had the statistics and the confidence, the ego remained average, Wesley says. "I remember one year we went up to play Louisiana Tech with Karl Malone. I just happened to go by Joe's room. He was in there reading his Bible. I went in and asked him what he was doing. He said his mom had started him reading different proverbs and scriptures. I don't remember which one exactly he was reading, but it said to let others boast for you, to stay away from wrong, to stay in the path of righteousness. No wonder he's the person he is."

A starter from his freshman year, Dumars averaged 26.4 points his junior season, 1983-84, enough to finish sixth in the NCAA Division I scoring race. Without a lot of talent to go with him, McNeese struggled somewhat in the Southland Conference. And while Dumars' reputation wasn't national, he did earn an invitation to the Olympic Trials spring of 1984, an indication that he was quietly starting to make a

His style is to make opponents work for their shots.

name for himself.

That fall, however, he encountered his first major difficulty. He was playing a pickup game the day before fall practice began when he broke the fifth metatarsal bone in his right foot. "They told me I could either keep it in a cast for three months, sit out the whole year and red shirt or have surgery," Dumars says.

As always, Dumars consulted his mother. "She is a very spiritual lady," he says, "and she gave me some spiritual guidance at the time. She just told me to keep the faith, and she said, 'All the doctors don't have all the answers.' I believed what she was saying and I truly believed I could

come back and play.

"So I chose none of the above. I told them, 'I am going to take this thing off and I am going to play in six weeks.' They told me, 'There is no way you are going to be able to play this year without staying in a permanent cast for three months.' They assured me I wouldn't be opening the season.

"At first, they put one of those permanent casts on my leg," Dumars says, "and I was going crazy. So I said, 'You have got to take that off and put something else on.' They put on one of those portable casts with a strap on it and said, 'You can take it off at night.' So after a week or so I

17

Joe at his parents' home in Natchitoches. (The Sporting News/Andrew Bernstein/NBA)

would sit on the edge of the bed putting my foot on the floor. Just had it touch the floor, and I started doing it and I gradually built up and started standing up and walking around. I would do that every night, and nobody would know I was doing it. I would close my dorm door and lock up and just kind of walk around in my room. And then I started running in place and exercising and jumping, and I did that for three weeks probably before anybody even knew it."

Dumars had forced his destiny. Instead of redshirting, or missing most of the season, he was ready to play when it began. "I came out and

told them I was ready," he says. "They were like, there is no way you can play. So I took it off and I started playing. That was five years ago. A guy looked at it after I started playing and he said the bone had healed and he couldn't believe it."

He went on to average 25.8 points his senior year and earned Southland Player of the Year honors as well as second-team mention on The Sporting News All-America team. Former University of Houston Coach Guy Lewis remembers coaching Dumars in a post-season all-star game that year. "I was really impressed with him," Lewis said. "The way he practiced, his court sense, the

way he handled himself."

Pro scouts had the same impressions, so Dumars, a four-time All-Southland selection, had enough confidence to go to New York for the 1985 NBA draft. "They had about 12 players up there," he says. "A couple of teams that went before Detroit had told me they would draft me, and when they didn't it was a little unnerving. It worked out well. When I initially came to Detroit I was wondering, why would they draft me? I knew they had three good guards here, and I wasn't too enthused about coming. But it was really a blessing in disguise."

The same low-key, hard-work

approach that worked so well in high school and college, did the trick again in Detroit. It wasn't long before rookie Joe Dumars had replaced veteran John Long in the starting lineup.

THE RING

Mr. Dumars would never volunteer the information, but if you ask enough questions, you'll find he served with General George Patton in World War II. Joe Dumars II was a mere 17 when he joined the Army in 1942. Two years later he found himself with a trucking unit in England, and by June 1944, he was swept up by that massive assault, the Normandy Invasion.

His task was to drive a gasoline tanker, the lifeline for Patton's famed tank corps. It was what you might call powder-keg duty. The Germans figured if they were going to stop the advancing allies, bombing and strafing the supply lines was the smart way. The Luftwaffe, at least what was left of it, turned its full force to this task.

Patton, on the other hand, was never the kind to wait around. Mr. Dumars remembers the general striking a proud figure and saying, "Hell, we ain't got nothing but blood and guts. So let's hit it! Hit it!"

Hit it they did. Rolling across Belgium, Patton's troops crossed the Rhine River ahead of orders, schedules, even maps. "He'd get in one of those tanks and be the head leader," Mr. Dumars says of Patton. "We got lost for three days. We overrun the map after we crossed the Rhine River."

With the Luftwaffe gunning for them, they did much of their moving at night. Mr. Dumars recalls driving in the blackness and stopping the truck to get out and feel the edge of the road to make sure he was still on track. Straying off the road into a minefield held a special terror for a gasoline tanker driver, nearly as much terror as a strafing.

"He didn't think he'd ever get back home," Ophelia Dumars says of her husband.

He returned from the war to life in Jim Crow America. But the private hurt of Joe Dumars II was much greater than his public one. His father, the original Joe Dumars, had two sons, one of whom he had kept with him. The other son, Joe Dumars II, was just two weeks old when the father sent him to be raised by his grandmother in Natchitoches.

The father never explained this action to the son. Joe Dumars II grew up never knowing why he had been rejected by his parents. Trying to gain an understanding of his personal life remained a torturous thing for him. The first step in healing the hurt came in July 1954, when he married Ophelia Jones. A few months later, Mr. Dumars went to work as a driver for a wholesale grocery company, beginning three decades of Herculean workdays.

Working as a driver in the rural South wasn't easy in those days, but Mr. Dumars' war experience had left him with an understated confidence. "Every day wasn't Sunday now, I can't say that," he says. "In those days, we had so much going between the races and everything." Yet he had a knack for getting the job done.

It helped that his wife was a religious person. Her spirituality eventually guided him to come to terms with his family's rejection. After his own religious conversion, Joe Dumars decided to simply accept what had happened and let it be. This explains, to some degree, why in 1963, after six children and five sons, Joe Dumars II was able to name his seventh child Joe Dumars III.

Mr. Dumars admits he was a demanding father, always pushing his children to do better in the hours and minutes he saw them around his work schedule. It's obvious today that he takes immense pride in the strong family he and his wife have built from the shattered one he grew out of.

His 1989 success has brought Joe into the spotlight. (The Sporting News/Andrew Bernstein/NBA)

Joe goes for Magic's hook against L.A.

"Out of the seven, every one of them, they don't mind work," he says. "Life is so short, you have so much you run into. You have to bring them up the right way."

Joe Dumars II stayed at his back-breaking schedule for 30 years. Then in 1985, during his son's rookie year in the NBA, Mr. Dumars began having blackouts. He was on the job when he had the most serious one. "He just kept blacking out," Ophelia Dumars says. "He had a blood pressure and a sugar problem he didn't know about. On that day, he had made a delivery to a store and was on his way back to the truck. He had been working that truck since September of '54. He had never been sick."

Struck by an acute diabetic reaction, Mr. Dumars fell gravely ill. To save his life, doctors eventually amputated both of his legs above the knees. Used to seeing their father so strong, the Dumars children were understandably devastated by his illness. Joe, caught in the schedule of his NBA rookie season, could do little more than phone for updates on his father's condition.

"All of us are aware of the price Dad paid every day," Mark Dumars says of his siblings. "I don't see any of us as rowdy type people. We were always quiet. It's kind of hard to let your parents down when they work so hard."

Mr. Dumars' days are up and down now. Some days his sickness gets the best of him. In addition to looking out for the grandchildren, Ophelia Dumars spends her time making sure her husband gets his medication and eats the right food.

As might be expected, Mr. Dumars derives immense pleasure from watching his son's televised basketball games. Sometimes the excitement gets to be too much, such as the Chicago series during last spring's playoffs, when he experienced chest pains and a shortness of breath. Fortunately, after that, the Lakers series was a sweep, and the tension eased.

"He loves watching the games," Joe Dumars says of his father. "He

lives for that. He never misses a game. He is sitting there right in front of the TV." In turn, Dumars says he draws inspiration from his father. For a Father's Day gift, Joe gave his dad his NBA championship ring.

"I'm thankful to be here," Mr. Dumars said just before Father's Day. "People come in the house and look at me in a kind of pitiful state. I tell them, 'Don't pity me.' I still got breath in the body and my family. You learn to take blows and hold your head up and keep going. Everything hasn't been peaches and cream in life, but you find some way around it to keep going."

THE PROFESSIONAL

From the high of earning a starting job in his rookie NBA season to the low of his father's illness, Joe Dumars has kept a steady course in pro basketball. Each year his role in the Pistons' offense has increased dramatically. With each season, he has played more minutes, taken more shots, scored more points (up from 9.2 points per game as a rookie to 17.2 last year) and played better defense.

Dumars broke his left hand last January and was sidelined for almost a month, but the first real setback in

Dantley and Dumars were close.

21

his professional career didn't come until a week after he returned to action, when the Pistons traded his friend and mentor, Adrian Dantley, to the Dallas Mavericks for forward Mark Aguirre. Dantley had come to the Pistons from the Utah Jazz before the 1986-87 season, and since that time, he and Dumars had become close friends. Like Dumars, Dantley is a quiet man, with a modest, conservative approach to life. With a dozen pro seasons in his experience, Dantley's nickname of "Teacher" was apt. There was much he taught the younger Dumars about coping with the lifestyle.

But Dantley also had a unique offensive style. One of the premier scorers in the game, he was used to getting the ball. And having been traded four times in his first four years in the NBA, he admitted that he trusted few people, particularly coaches and management types. He had been the team's leading scorer in 1986-87, when the Pistons advanced to the conference finals, and again in 1987-88, as the Pistons extended the Lakers to seven games before losing the championship series.

But as General Manager Jack McCloskey explained later, the Pistons had become a divided team during the 1988-89 season. Word of a trade had been coursing for months around the organization. Then it seemed to be dead, and that's why Dumars was stunned to learn, in the midst of a West Coast road trip, that the deal had gone through.

"He was real hurt by that, real hurt," Dumars' best friend, John Wesley, says of the Dantley trade.

Throughout his career, Dumars has quietly amazed the sportswriters covering the Pistons. But never more so than in the aftermath of the trade. As Charlie Vincent of the *Detroit Free Press* said one day while watching a Pistons practice, some type of reaction would be only human. Most humans, in fact, might engage in a bit of pouting, or at least wear their emotions on their sleeve.

Dumars, however, never allowed so much as a ripple to enter his businesslike approach to the game.

Joe found solace in his parents' backyard. (The Sporting News/Andrew Bernstein/NBA)

His response was almost superhuman.

"It is imperative that a person be in control of himself," he says when asked about his response. "I learned discipline from a very early age. You have to have it to be successful for the long term. If you're undisciplined I don't know if you will be able to maintain success over a long period of time. I realized when Adrian's situation went down that it was paramount that I stay as professional as possible and not let it affect me emotionally. You can't get that

wrapped up into something that affects your job. You can't bring personal things on the job."

Pistons management made no attempt to explain the trade to Dumars, a move that might have enraged other players. But McCloskey and Coach Chuck Daly had read Dumars correctly. "Nobody came up and said anything," Dumars says. "Nobody had to. I am glad no one came to me because I don't want them to think I'm one of those guys they have to pamper. I don't want that. I could care less about having

my ego stroked or pampering me. This is the real world. You have to accept things and you have to go on. Every time something happens in your life that is not what you would want it to be, you are not always going to have someone to pat you on your back and say it's great. You know, my dad worked for thirty years on that truck and when he had a bad day there was no one patting him on his back saying, 'You know, Joe, it's going to be okay.' You have to bear with it and go on. Nobody has to come to me and do that. I can

understand life and I can understand what goes on in the world whether I like it or not. And I can accept it and go on. "

The effect of the trade was not without irony. Because Aguirre was a better passer than people realized (Dantley was notorious for holding the ball while he set up his post moves), Dumars became more involved in the offense. Throughout the final third of the season, Dumars found himself taking more shots. He even told Dantley this in a phone conversation. And Chuck Daly noticed that the

shooting guards for other teams had increasing trouble defending Dumars.

The situation culminated in his 42-point performance against Cleveland in April, the game that clinched the divisional title for the Pistons. In the third quarter alone, Dumars hit for a club-record 24 points. A team of many looks and weapons, the Pistons had suddenly found a new force to unleash.

"I mean it was mindboggling," Chuck Daly said afterward. "I've never really seen him do that before, take over the game quite like that.

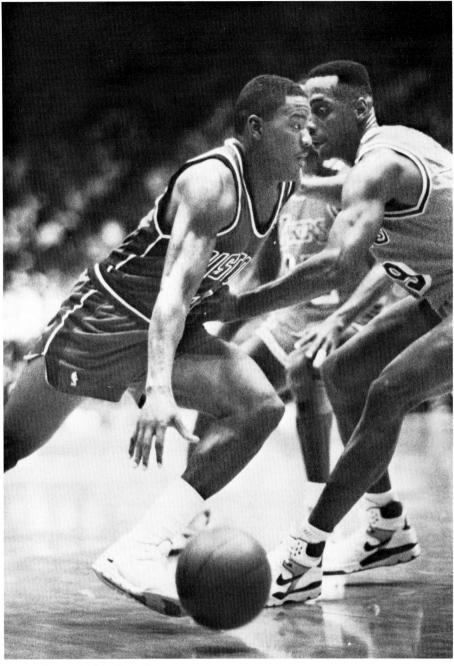

Dumars loves playing the point.

"Isiah's a great player," Dumars said not long after coming to the team. "He's my favorite NBA player. I like to see him with the ball. I feel he can create a lot of things. I can do those things, too, but I feel I have to give him first crack at it when we're paired."

At the same time, Dumars admits he isn't the type of person to command the spotlight. A big scorer in college, he found immediate playing time in the pros by developing as an exceptional defender. Yet even his defensive play wasn't the kind that draws attention. He was overlooked his first three years as a pro before being named to the league's all-defensive first team in 1989.

"The type of defense that I play is not the type that gambles a lot," he says. "I'm not going to do a lot of flashy things on defense. I am not going to gamble on steals and blocked shots. I am not going to do a lot of those things. I play containment defense. I try to contain the person, make them shoot more than they want to shoot to get their points. If he gets 30 points, he has to shoot 28 times, or 29 times to get 30 points. If a person is gambling a lot I figure he is going to get beat three or four times where a guy gets easy buckets."

Dumars' emergence last season as an offensive player brought more questions about his role. Does Isiah cramp his style? he was asked late in the season. With a team as talented as the Pistons, you have to play roles, he replied. "I think I do my role pretty well."

Yet it's significant that the Pistons eventually reached their championship by blurring the roles. Isiah and Dumars became interchangeable. More and more during the stretch, Thomas would move to shooting guard and Dumars would run the point.

Both players have said they liked the reversal, Thomas because of the opportunity to shoot more, Dumars because he likes the responsibility. "That's like being in charge of Church's Fried Chicken," he says of playing point guard. "You got to run

We've been leaning that way for a long time, six or eight weeks now, and we've been going more and more to him."

"Joe can shoot from anywhere on the court at any time," Pistons center Bill Laimbeer said after that game. "He's always going to play in the shadow of Isiah's name. So be it. Maybe that's good for him. Maybe that will take a little of the star pressure off him and he can go about and do his job and win games for the Pistons. But we know how capable Joe is. I know every other player in

the league knows how capable Joe is. He's never going to get that name recognition of a Bird or an Isiah or a Magic."

There is something in this last statement that doesn't sit well with Dumars, mainly because it implies that there is some aspect of the game that he can't handle.

During his senior year in college, Dumars was asked which pro player he most admired. His answer: Isiah Thomas. Dumars' coming to the Pistons, however, raised questions about his duplicating Isiah.

the show. And when I move over to point I know I have to run the show. I like that. I like the idea of let me see how I can push it in there. But you have to have the personnel to do it, and Isiah and I are interchangeable enough where it suits us perfectly."

Playing point guard for a team like the Pistons is the ultimate basketball challenge because there are so many options, he says. "It's like you have to know how to push the right buttons to get all four guys flowing. I like being out front with this team."

Beyond that, point guard is the ultimate learning experience, Dumars says. "I guarantee you Magic Johnson is still learning the point guard spot. I guarantee you he doesn't know everything, and he will probably tell you he is still learning. You can never stop learning because so many different things happen in every game. So many things happen every time, you have to learn."

DOWN ON THE BAYOU

Learning is a big part of Dumars' life, and it goes beyond basketball. He is 15 hours shy of a degree from McNeese State, which he is determined to get. It's just that the NBA playoffs have occupied the past few summers, he says "Summer school starts at the end of May. Little did I know that we would become so good that I never would get home in time for summer school anymore."

He plans to go further and get a graduate degree, because he's fascinated by much more than basketball. By world affairs. And real estate. And banking. "I want to know about the world beyond basketball," he says.

The culture of his home state is another part of this fascination. Dumars and his wife, Debbie, who is also a Louisiana native, will live the off season in Lake Charles, on the Gulf Coast, where he went to college at McNeese State. "Louisiana is different than any other state in this country," Dumars says. "North Louisiana is more the Texas, hillbilly type. South Louisiana is all the Cajun people. I grew up in north Louisiana,

but in south Louisiana I've learned the Cajun culture. People are very different down there. The north Louisiana people are Texas types, more conservative. The Cajun type people are more liberal and more Mardi Gras, more, 'Let's have a good time.' It's two different worlds and I think I got the best of both of them. I think that's how I got my strict disciplinary personality, from growing up in that area. Everybody thinks along those lines—'Don't get out of line too much.' "

He says he has learned to be comfortable in Detroit, but back home, he says, "I can totally let my

"And when I move over to point I know I have to run the show. I like that. I like the idea of letting me see how I can push it in there. But you have to have the personnel to do it, and Isiah and I are interchangeable enough where it suits us perfectly."

—Joe Dumars

guard down. All of my guard. Here, I am comfortable, but I still have a shield up. Because I didn't grow up around these people, and they didn't know what my life was like growing up. Not that I am saying life was so

tough. But, when you're around people that grew up in the same type of situation that you did, there is no explaining. A lot of times your actions are understood without you ever having to explain."

His hometown has done everything imaginable to return Dumars' affection. The City of Natchitoches honored him last July with Joe Dumars Appreciation Day, an extravaganza that included a parade, a luncheon, a spot on the city's Walk of Fame and even the renaming of a city park for him, all of which left Dumars feeling extremely uncomfortable. Between events, he spent his time hiding in his old room at his parents' house, and his speech at the luncheon was the shortest one all day.

"The most important thing about today," he told the crowd, "is that these people have something to be proud of. I'm just the vehicle. I can't get caught up in what I'm doing. I know 70 million people in 60 different countries watch the NBA Finals, so I know that's important. But me, I'm not that important. Twenty years ago, somebody did the same thing, and 20 years from now, somebody else will still be doing it. I'm just passing through."

Perhaps Dumars could offer the rest of the world a primer on how to pursue excellence while keeping your humility about you. Like his mother told him long ago, Joe Dumars is special. Perhaps the most special thing about him is his mix of confidence and humility. In many athletes, those properties seem mutually exclusive. The confidence they have on court can translate into a humongous ego once they step off.

How can you have both confidence and humility? you ask Joe.

"In life," he says, "very few things are important. A lot of things are relevant. But very few are really important."

And what is important?

"Family," he says. "Nothing is more important than that."

Spider and Zeke get a feel for the prize.

The Year Of The Broom

Y ou looking for drama?
You looking for that basketball junkie fix, that nail-biting, late-game tension?

Look someplace else, chump.

This one was about grit and mysticism and destiny and drive. And craziness. A lot of craziness.

This was a slit-your-wrist-if-you-lose kind of proposition. They had too much at stake. Seriously. If they hadn't won the title, it wouldn't be hard to imagine Zeke and Laimbeer doing weave drills in the looney bin.

Drama was a disease.

All they really wanted to do was dance. To power in and possess the trophy. And dance.

They stalked it like a pack of crazed beggars, led by the prophet Isiah, the little dude beset by a weird vision. He had a dream—he nurtured that dream—of the perfect championship. Sweep. Sweep. Sweep. Sweep. All the way to the title. Kept it fresh in his mind every day, because it tortured him all night long, kept him twisting and turning. Kept him up late.

Why the hell he wanted it so badly even he couldn't tell you. He wasn't so much a point guard as he was a Charles Manson. A weird little dude. Would do anything to get that ring.

And the Pistons? They weren't a team so much as they were a cult. The Cult of the Broom. Sweep. Sweep. Sweep.

Laimbeer and Mahorn were the Sergeants at Arms.

Joe Dumars the Minister of Defense.

The rest of them were a loose band of vagabonds. Vinnie. Buddha. Worm. Spider. And the rest. No wonder Rolling Stone posed them in black leather and biker gear.

Chuck Daly was a sort of scoutmaster to keep 'em in line.

As Isiah Thomas explained, they didn't want to fool with the 1989 regular season; they just wanted to go directly to the Finals again where they could correct their mistakes.

Still, they wandered a bit and at times seemed lost. But in the end they found it. Sweep. Sweep. Sweep. The Year of the Broom.

When they finally got their golden prize, the results were almost obscene. They kissed it and sweet-talked it and licked it and danced with it.

Anybody who had ever heard anything about false idols had to be worried about lightning striking the locker room that night in Los Angeles.

The Bad Boys had lusted after this prize.

And watching them get it, you had to be worried about 'em. Would they ever want anything this Bad again?

THE PATTERN

As many championship stories do, this one begins at the end of the previous season. The Pistons had held a 3-2 lead in games heading to Los Angeles for the last two games of the 1988 Finals. And then they lost two in LA., leaving them with this deep-six kind of emptiness.

That transformed into an air of impatience hovering over the opening of training camp in the fall. As Isiah Thomas explained, they didn't want to fool with the 1988-89 regular season; they just wanted to go directly to the Finals again where they could correct their mistakes.

Still, as training camps go, it was a good one. Plenty of hustle, plenty of hoops. Not much rust on the pipes. They came out of it like a team headed for the Finals. The troubles, however, began almost immediately.

Over the summer, NBA Properties had released its "Bad Boys" video, and where that image had dogged at their heels in the past, it crawled right up into their laps at the start of the year. It wasn't long before the Bad Boys lap dog threatened to run the show. Perhaps, in retrospect, that is the most amazing thing about the Detroit Pistons' championship. They achieved it while running an entertainment business.

For a time, it seemed, they were first and foremost "The Bad Boys." They had their posters and their posed magazine shots and book deals and endorsements. It made you wonder how they could remember to play basketball. That's where Chuck Daly came into the picture. The Daly reminder.

Right from the start, the NBA powers that be took a dim view of Detroit's modus operandi. In an exhibition game against the Washington Bullets, played in Baltimore, the baddest of the boys, Pistons forward Rick Mahorn, and Bullets center Dave Feitl squared off and battled. Then, after being ejected, they went at it again in the locker room, where seven security guards did their best to pry Mahorn off Feitl.

The NBA's vice president for operations, Rod Thorn, fined Mahorn $5,000 and Feitl $3,000.

The first of the season unfolded as a blueprint from there. With each game, the pattern became more discernable. Chuck Daly had this incredible bench, and whenever he needed something, he went to it. Usually, he found what he was looking for. They walloped Chicago, 107-94, on the road to open the regular season. The second quarter featured a confrontation between Isiah and Bulls center Bill Cartwright. No fisticuffs. But plenty of woofing and icy stares.

The next night, Saturday, November 5, they officially opened business at the Palace of Auburn Hills, entertaining, then disenfranchising, the Charlotte Hornets, one of two new expansion teams in the league.

The revealing game, however, came the next week, when a retooled Atlanta, featuring newly acquired center Moses Malone and guard Reggie Theus, came to the Palace. The Pistons trailed 79-66 early in the fourth quarter, as Daly benched Adrian Dantley and went with Isiah, John Salley, Vinnie Johnson, James Edwards and Dennis Rodman.

Using its speed and defensive prowess, this second unit froze the Hawks for six minutes and pulled within one at 79-78. On that momentum, the Pistons won in overtime, 101-95.

"We got in a big hole early in the fourth quarter," Daly explained

afterward, "so I said what the heck, let's go with our speed team. What's the old adage in sports? Hustle and enthusiasm can overcome anything. We weren't getting the effort from some players so I went with a different lineup. If players don't respond and really work hard on defense, I'll make moves sooner."

Asked about his time on the bench, Dantley replied it didn't matter. "It's good we have a team which can use different guys on different nights," he said. "Whoever plays good stays in. That's a coach's decision and it's good as long as we win."

As long as we win?

It was irritating little phrases like

Asked about Rodman, Dantley said, "I'm not envious if Rodman gets in there a minute. That's a coach's decision."

that that ultimately got Dantley in trouble. He had said the same thing about Game Seven of the Finals against the Lakers, when he had been benched in favor of Rodman. The circumstances revealed a stiff uneasiness between player and coach.

The Atlanta game was noteworthy for one other reason. The league fined Mahorn $1,000 for flagrant fouls. That Friday night, the Pistons traveled to Boston and won. Detroit center Bill Laimbeer and Celtics center Robert Parish had a little shoving match, resulting in a $1,500 fine for Parish, $1,000 for Laimbeer.

"I'm not going to pay it," Laimbeer told reporters (he did). "I'm going to appeal that as soon as I can. It's a bad decision. They're singling out Ricky and me to try and intimidate us."

The Pistons, meanwhile, had run their record to 6-0 with a 108-99 road win over Dallas. Dantley and Dallas forward Mark Aguirre had collided

early in the game, when Dantley drew a charging foul. Aguirre's elbow struck Dantley, smashing his lip and knocking loose three teeth. A later diagnosis revealed Dantley's upper jaw was fractured. It was a most fortuitous little collision.

They continued on their Southwest road swing, claiming wins in Phoenix and San Antonio, before dropping their first game in Houston. They picked up a win in Charlotte but returned home for a disastrous loss in the Palace to New York, 133-111. Back from injury, Dantley scored 25, but Daly was left fuming at the lack of defensive intensity.

"We just broke down mentally," Salley suggested afterward.

At 9-2, they faced a Thanksgiving weekend rematch with the Lakers. The Golden Boys came to the Palace on Kareem Abdul-Jabbar's farewell tour. The Pistons honored the 42-year-old center in a pre-game ceremony, then the two teams went at it brutally. It was a tight game, eventually won by the Pistons, 102-99, when Magic Johnson's desperation shot missed at the buzzer. Rodman had gotten a key offensive rebound with 15 seconds left to put the Pistons over the top.

"We just wanted to prove we could beat these guys, whether it was the Finals or not," Rodman said afterward. A rebounder and a defender, he was Daly's type of player. Already it was apparent he would get more and more playing time in key situations, much of it at Dantley's expense.

Asked about Rodman, Dantley said, "I'm not envious if Rodman gets in there a minute. That's a coach's decision." But appearances suggested different.

Midway through the third quarter against Los Angeles, Dantley had gone to the bench, where he sat quietly until nearly three minutes into the fourth quarter, when Daly, who had been twisting and turning and pacing on the sideline, suddenly stopped and ran down to Dantley.

"Let's go! Let's go!" the coach, motioning toward the floor, shouted to the 33-year-old forward.

Daly would have preferred that Dantley become immediately charged with enthusiasm and hustle into the game. But the veteran rose deliberately, broke out of his warm-up jacket and moved at his own peculiar pace to the scorer's table. His face was frozen into a blankness as it had been all night, perhaps for all of his life.

Moments later, Dantley had the ball 15 feet deep into the left corner. He bent at the waist and began a slow-motion rocker step, pawing his right foot back and forth on the floor. The motion was surrealistically slow, and this unsettled his defender, A.C. Green, who stepped back to prevent one of Dantley's patented drives.

Dantley paused to consider his options another moment, then to everyone's surprise he decided to take advantage of what the defender had given him and swished a swift set shot. "I work at my own pace," he explained later. "My game is trying to lull my guy to sleep, then exploding on him."

For 13 seasons, the 6'4" Dantley had been striking dread into his opponents with that same blank game face and his nearly indefensible offensive skills. He was what you might call the Clint Eastwood of the NBA, a High Plains Drifter in the low post. On many nights the only thing that seemed to be missing was a cheroot in his teeth and a serape to cover his shooting hand.

The comparison to Clint pleased Dantley. "Eastwood is one of my favorite guys," he said. "I've seen just about all of his movies."

Not lost in this comparison is the fact that Eastwood's High Plains Drifter persona is a loner. Throughout his long NBA career, Dantley had been a loner, too, often leaving in his wake puzzled teammates who claimed not to understand him.

That was particularly true with the Utah Jazz, where he spent seven seasons building his reputation as both a scorer and a difficult guy. Former Jazz teammate Thurl Bailey once said of Dantley, "I think, over my years of playing, he is probably the most complex guy as far as breaking

through his personality and getting to know the real A.D., which I don't think anybody will ever know "

Dantley readily admitted that he had always been slow to trust people. "I don't really think of myself as a loner," he said. "People misinterpret my face. I'm leery of people. I'm always trying to figure them out, decide where they're coming from. I

guess I tend to stare right at them instead of smiling."

Dantley's difficult reputation had subsided substantially after he was traded to Detroit in 1987. In the past, he had seemed adamant that his scoring skills should make him the focus of any team's offense. But he knew the Pistons were too talented and diverse for that. He conceded his

The Pistons won a sloppy rematch with the Lakers at Thanksgiving.

lesser role in Detroit was a difficult adjustment, but his past successes helped, Dantley said. "I've experienced a lot of things. Three scoring titles. I've averaged over 30 points for four years.

"It doesn't bother me now. I'm not expected to score here like I did previously. We have balanced scoring and a depth of talent." More important for him now than scoring, is winning, he said. "Everybody wants to win; everybody wants to play well. A lot of times those things don't happen together."

Although Dantley admitted to wondering about it privately from time to time, he said he has never questioned Daly about keeping him on the bench in the last minutes of Game Seven of the 1988 Finals while Rodman played. For his part, Daly said he didn't care what Dantley thought of Game Seven. Daly said he had gone with a quick lineup that had almost wiped out the Lakers' big lead and pulled off a miracle.

Despite this tension between the coach and the team's leading scorer, the Pistons had been winning. They had faced a heavy road schedule and a host of nagging injuries. Backup center James Edwards had a sprained left ankle. Mahorn's perennial back problems returned again. Joe Dumars had a sprained right ankle. Dantley had back spasms and an aching jaw. They went to Indiana with only nine of 12 on the roster able to play. Which helped explain their poor shooting and late loss to the Pacers, 107-98. Even with the defeat, the Pistons had scorched the league in November, finishing the month at 11-3, strong enough to earn Daly Coach-of-the-Month honors.

Playing well and winning, as Dantley said, don't always happen together.

DOWNTURN

From there, the momentum shifted, making December uneasy and January downright strange. The first controversy came when Laimbeer complained to the Detroit papers that the fans in the Palace

Vinnie goes for the loose ball in the opening home game at the Palace.

were the quietest in the league. That brought an outburst of protest. It was pointed out that when the Pistons played downtown in Cobo Arena in previous seasons, the smaller crowds seemed rowdier. And later, when the Pistons called the Pontiac Silverdome home, the throng of 20,000 to 38,000 had been deafening. In comparison, the 21,000 plus fans at the Palace were just warming to the new arena.

Many fans were irked by

Laimbeer's suggestion that the crowd was too well-heeled to be spirited. The remarks prompted Leon "The Barber" Bradley, Detroit's senior boogey man who strides onto the floor during timeouts to pump up the crowd, to tell *The Detroit News*: "And the players complain. Bill Laimbeer made me so mad when he said the fans don't cheer. Look at the price you pay. It's gotta be an upscale crowd. They don't cheer, they

Dantley moved to tenth on the NBA all-time scoring list before the trade. (Einstein photo)

applaud. But [Pistons' management] got what they wanted [a new arena in the suburbs], and they better keep winning." The impatience factor, it seemed, loomed everywhere. The problem would work itself out, but not immediately.

Milwaukee blew them out, 109-84, December 6, as the Pistons played terribly, shooting 40 percent from the floor and scoring only 31 points in the second half, the lowest total in the history of the franchise.

"Maybe it's me," Daly said afterward. "Maybe I want too much. I am looking at it through a magnifying glass wanting perfection."

The next night, Dumars held Michael Jordan to a season-low 18 points as Detroit beat the Bulls at the Palace. On paper, things looked

great. They stood 16-4 after facing a heavy road schedule. Their success had been sparked by the quiet factor, Dumars, who was playing well offensively and defensively. "Joe started the season on fire," Daly said. "And what makes it tough is that he can't take a night off defensively."

Still, the expectations were high, the uneasiness growing with each day. The road schedule figured largely in the negative mood. Everywhere they went, particularly in the Central Division, the Bad Boys drew heat from the crowds. Every newspaper in every city seemed to be running features on the NBA's Darth Vaders. "There is nothing you can do about it," Laimbeer said. "That is their way to promote the game and get more people to come in here and boo

us. I don't mind." In fact, the Pistons had prospered on the road, another trend that would become increasingly important in this year of brooms. "We know in the backs of our minds how successful we've been, especially on the road," Laimbeer said. "We also know that we don't have the type of team that's going to bury people. A lot of our games are going to be decided down the stretch, and we're always prepared for that."

Somehow, it was no surprise that when their schedule eased in December and January with more home games, their troubles deepened. A week later, in mid-December, they suffered their first back-to-back losses of the season, to Milwaukee again, then to surprising Cleveland.

That week trade rumors had begun swirling everywhere. John Salley, Vinnie Johnson, William Bedford, Darryl Dawkins, rookies Michael Williams and Fennis Dembo—all were mentioned. Perhaps that spurred them on. They rolled out of the losses with a run of winning, dropping one road game at New York, before finishing the month at 9-4, 20-7 on the season.

"People had better be glad we are winning," Thomas told reporters. "In other words, shut up. Be happy with the win."

January, however, would not be a happy time. Dantley fell into a mild slump in late December and early January, and Rodman's playing time increased. Over 10 games, Dantley averaged a mere 13.4 points. Even worse, he was just about all of the Pistons' inside game. When Dantley wasn't driving and drawing fouls, the Pistons' offense struggled and he didn't go to the free throw line as much.

Daly speculated for reporters that perhaps Dantley's jaw injury had left him gun shy. "Maybe Adrian became more of a perimeter player after he got hurt, I don't know," Daly said. "He took an awful belt in the mouth. It might be a subconscious thing."

Also somewhat disappointing had been the individual play of Thomas, Edwards, who seemed so potent in

Laimbeer gets heated against Houston.

> **"People had better be glad we are winning. In other words, shut up. Be happy with the win."**
>
> **—Isiah Thomas**

last year's playoffs, Salley, and Vinnie Johnson. Thomas speculated that the team was struggling offensively because it was playing well defensively. Isiah said he wanted to sustain the running game to keep things moving. Moving up the tempo was an obvious solution, but it took the team further away from Dantley's halfcourt post game. The team stalled on this issue, headed in two different directions.

"There are not a lot of happy campers here right now," a team official said in early January.

Over the coming weeks, the issue would bring a public focus on the relationship between Thomas and Dantley. While Dantley was close with the quiet Dumars, he and Thomas were worlds apart. Neither player wanted to make much of their differences, and Dantley scoffed at reports of a problem.

"This is not A.D.'s team, it's Isiah's team," he said. "I'm playing my role. That would have bothered me when I was 27 or 28 years old. I probably wouldn't have gone for it. But this stage of my career is fascinating in itself. Since coming to Detroit I'm more of a perimeter player than I was in Utah. Detroit is more of a perimeter team. I'm our one focus inside."

Still, scoring was tremendously important to Dantley. It is his purpose in his professional life. He readily pointed out that most teams evaluate their players on statistics, and contract negotiations are based on statistics. And perhaps that was the underlying problem: Thomas' contract was renegotiated in the offseason, raising his salary to $2 million annually, up from $750,000. Dantley

Mahorn drew the league's attention early and often.

was paid about $900,000. Still, he flatly denied any problem. "All of us guys get along real well together," he said. "When we play the Bullets in Washington, we'll have six to seven guys at my mom's house. In Atlanta, we've all gone to John Salley's house."

If the team's talent cuts into his playing minutes, Dantley said he would accommodate that, "but for me to be effective, I have to get more minutes."

By then, however, it was really too late. General Manager Jack McCloskey had become convinced

the team was irreparably divided. His thoughts were confirmed when the Pistons hit the skids in January. A weaker executive might have sat back and watched the team self-destruct. After all, the decision to trade Dantley was a tough one. He was a popular player with the fans, and even though the Pistons were struggling, they still had one of the best records in the league. But McCloskey and Daly had worked too hard, too long to let the situation get away from them when they were so close to success.

Over the first 27 days of January,

In January, Cleveland held power in the Central Division.

the Pistons went 6-6. All the while, one event after another added to the turmoil. First, assistant coach Dick Versace, who communicated well with Dantley, took the job as head coach of the Indiana Pacers, leading Detroit to hire Brendan Suhr, Atlanta's director of scouting, as a chief assistant. Then, on January 11, Dumars broke a bone in his left hand during a 100-93 loss to the Knicks in the Palace. The injury sidelined him a month, and the team signed journeyman guard Pace Mannion as a replacement. A day later, center William Bedford returned to a drug treatment center in California, in yet another attempt to cure his cocaine addiction. He had hoped to return to the team before Christmas but had again failed the terms of his treatment.

As Dantley and the team struggled offensively, his face seemed to freeze even more. The media began to interpret his actions as pouting, and the trade rumors began circulating. Asked if he shouldn't show more leadership and enthusiasm, Dantley said, "I try to concentrate on the game. A lot of that rah-rah stuff is good. A lot of it is phony. Some players like to do it for the fans. That's okay when it's done for the fans. We are in the entertainment business.

"As for Detroit, there are guys on our team to take care of the rah-rah, like John Salley. I have enough trouble going to bed after the games. I usually don't get to sleep before 5 a.m. If I got up for the game, I'd probably never get to sleep."

He admitted his attitude was a carryover from his early seasons in the league, when he was traded often. "It's a business," he said. "I learned it early. I was traded three times in three years. People say I have a problem getting close to management and coaches. But I've seen too many situations where they say they're not going to trade a player, then the next day he's gone. I just don't open up my arms to people. I don't tell them all of my business. A lot of coaches probably didn't like that about me."

Dantley, however, denied that he had an attitude problem, just a very private personality. "I don't think I'm any different than I've always been," he said. "I talk to people, I try to respect people. People just want to know about me. And because I don't let them know about me, I've got a bad attitude. I'm strange.... But I don't think I'm any different. Maybe I am mellowed out a little bit—I don't know —but I doubt it."

Finally Dantley found his range for 35 points, and they beat Washington January 13. Then he scored 24 that Sunday afternoon to become the 10th all-time leading scorer in league history, but the Pistons still lost to Milwaukee. The next night, they struggled in the first half against Boston in the Palace, bringing Daly to explode in the locker room at the half. "He started hollering and screaming so much that we all got this scared look on our faces," Salley said. Not given to outbursts, the 58-year-old Daly had shocked his players. They came out in the second half and fried the Celtics for a 96-87 win. From there, they won two more at home before dropping a 112-99 decision to the Celtics in Boston Garden, a game in which Dantley scored just seven points. Trying to get some steadiness to their play, Daly took to drilling fundamentals lightly in practice. At 58, the coach was too mature to panic. "I don't know if there is anything wrong with the offense," he told the beat writers. "I think everybody in the league is playing better defense. That's a fact, and I think it's going to continue that way."

They blew an 18-point lead against Golden State in the Palace on Janaury 22, but came back to win it at the wire. "If we had lost this game, I wouldn't have shown my face for these next two weeks," Rodman said afterward.

Daly was glum. "We're just not playing well together," the coach said. "Basic selfish problems are what I see. Until we resolve them, we're not going to be the team we were in the past."

McCloskey, too, was angry and

Neither Daly not the fans were sure what to make of things. (Einstein photo)

Every game, it seemed, was a battle.

Controversy seemed to follow Laimbeer.

met with the team immediately after the game, letting the players know he wasn't happy. The next day, the Detroit papers featured a trade rumor sending Dantley and Michael Williams to Portland for forward Kiki Vandeweghe and center Steve Johnson. The Pistons, however, didn't have the room in their salary cap to accommodate Vandeweghe's $1.05 million contract.

A piece of good news followed the same day, as late fan voting pushed Thomas ahead of Cleveland point guard Mark Price in the balloting for the All-Star game starting lineup. Appropriately, the Cavaliers came to the Palace for a battle the next game. Cleveland had a comfortable lead when center Brad Daugherty punched Laimbeer in the throat. As referee Darren Stafford tried to separate them, Laimbeer retaliated, landing a solid punch to Daugherty's jaw. Both were ejected, and with Daugherty's absence, the Pistons almost erased a 13-point Cleveland lead in the fourth quarter.

The Cavs, however, escaped 80-79, giving them a five-game lead over Detroit in the Central Division

Daly was glum. "We're just not playing well together," the coach said. "Basic selfish problems are what I see. Until we resolve them, we're not going to be the team we were in the past."

standings. "Somewhere along the line we lost something," Daly said afterward, "and we're not playing as well as we did last season. The game is simple, but the people are complex. We have some conflicts going."

A lot of them were with Rod Thorn's office. Once again, the league came down hard on fighting. Laimbeer was fined approximately $12,500, Daugherty $10,900, and both players were suspended for one

Rodman was too good to keep on the bench.

game, a move that wrecked Laimbeer's streak of playing 685 games without a miss.

The Pistons, without doubt, were a physical team. McCloskey said it was their style to play that way, and it was the officials' job to call fouls. But the fines made Laimbeer and Mahorn increasingly paranoid. They thought the league was out to get them. "I am not a dirty player and never tried to hurt anybody," Laimbeer told reporters. "That image was started by the press in Boston and has been promoted by the league."

Cleveland General Manager Wayne Embry fumed about the marketing of Bad Boys T-shirts. "Let's face it," he said. "Laimbeer and Mahorn are cheap shot artists. They deliberately try to hurt people, and that's not how the game is supposed to be played. There is no place in the NBA for these tactics."

Things strangely righted themselves from that point. They went on a seven-game winning streak that began with a blowout of Sacramento in the Palace in late January and ended suitably enough with a road win against Sacramento just after Valentine's Day.

Despite this good run and the season of hearts and cupids, things were hardly kissy in Motown.

MAKING A MOVE

Why are big trades always cast as "blockbusters"? Whose block gets busted anyway? The talk of trade in those intervening two weeks had an ebb and flow to it. Dantley for Aguirre. First it was on, then it was off. Finally, unexpectedly, it happened. A blockbuster.

In the days before it was sprung upon them, both players had the opportunity to talk about it. Aguirre, who was having trouble with his teammates and the Dallas fans, fled from it. "Have a nice day," he told reporters as he exited the locker room.

Dantley offered his game face. "They think I was trouble and they're going to trade for Mark Aguirre?" he asked incredulously, then had second

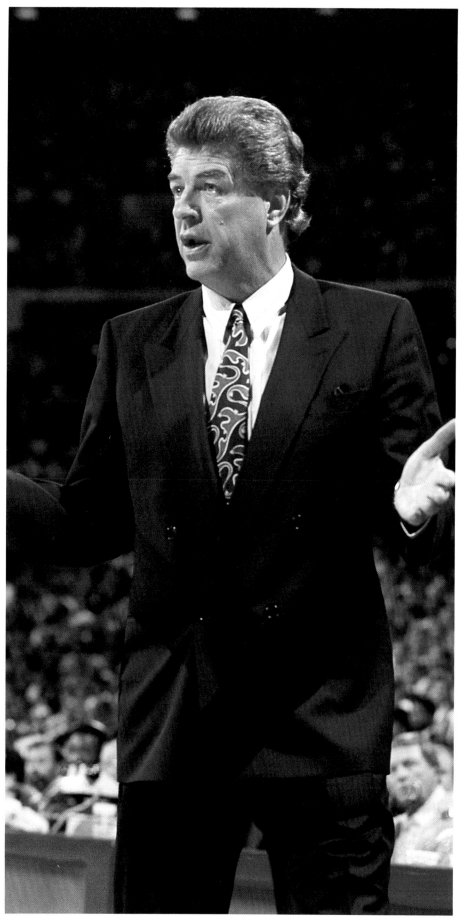

Daly wondered if he wasn't too much of a perfectionist.

39

thoughts. "Aw, it's not fair to say that. I don't know him. I only heard the rumors. I know how those things can be. Aguirre's a good player. I do know that. And he's got a hard elbow, too."

Dantley said he didn't want to be traded, but even as he toned down his pouting, even as Chuck Daly announced the team had returned to playoff form, the deal was being done.

The night before it went down, the Pistons took it to the Magic-less Lakers in the Forum, 111-103. Dumars had returned from injury, the team's spirits had buoyed, Dantley had headed out of his slump.

Which explains why he was caught off-guard by it. He balked, and at first refused to report to Dallas. His mother blamed Thomas and told reporters Isiah had instigated the deal to get his boyhood friend, Aguirre, to the Pistons. Thomas flatly denied any such arrangement, but regardless, he was handed the responsibility for making it work.

Aguirre, for his part, was elated. The number-one pick in the 1981 draft, he had played well for Dallas for seven seasons yet had acquired a tarnished image at the same time. In short, his teammates said that he was selfish, that he didn't always play hard. They bid him a rather public good riddance.

Magic Johnson, also a good friend of Aguirre's, once pointed out that carrying the load of team leadership was not Aguirre's strength. He would fit in better on a team where leadership pressures were spread out, Johnson said.

In Dallas, Aguirre had been a big part of the franchise, and had taken the team to the 1988 Western Conference finals. The pressure in Dallas had been unrealistic, Aguirre said not long after coming to Detroit. "I had to carry the team to the Finals. That's what I had to do. I tried to the best of my ability, and it didn't happen. But we did get extremely close. I wasn't able to play

comfortably. Now I'm here with the Pistons and I'm able to play comfortably. The offense is not as much concentrated on me, but I am able to contribute to a better team and that makes me happy."

Dantley was anything but. In a sense, the rest of the season would be cast as a debate. Detroit had given the 33-year-old Dantley plus the next year's first-round draft pick for the 29-year-old Aguirre. Was the trade good or bad? The players were very similar, both post-up types, both used to getting the ball. Would Aguirre show the spoiled act that had turned off the people in Dallas? Would he accept sharing time with the incredible rebounding, defensive machine, Dennis Rodman?

Surprisingly, Aguirre did. He came to Detroit in terrible shape. At 6'6", he had always had a weight problem, his poundage rising and falling between 232 and 250 and above. McCloskey had heard the stories about Aguirre and had some fears about his effect on the team. But the general manager was also confident in the leadership provided by Thomas, Laimbeer, Mahorn and Johnson. He mentioned to them his concerns about Aguirre.

Shortly after Aguirre's arrival, he and the four had a dinner "business" meeting. There, the expectations and guidelines were stated clearly and succinctly. "It was funy," Thomas said later after the meeting. "Mark hardly had a chance to eat. We put the spotlight on him, and we told him, 'This is how we do things with the Detroit Pistons.'

"At one point, Mark looked at me like he wanted to say: 'I'm your friend, Isiah. Tell these guys I'm O.K.' But I couldn't say anything. We're friends, but the team comes first. The most important thing we have around here is freedom, and the guys had some things they wanted to get off their chest.

"Actually, what happened to Mark happens to any new guy who joins this team. We've got some strong-willed guys who aren't going to let anyone mess us up. If push comes to shove, we'll mess them up first."

Once the Pistons' momentum got going, it was tough to stop.

Dumars broke his hand in January.

Nothing else had to be said. There was, however, a bruising demonstration of defense by Rodman and Mahorn in one of the early practices, but that was mostly a joke, used for publicity purposes.

Mark Aguirre had been rejected by his former team, and his reputation wasn't exactly good at the moment. He wanted to fit in.

Detroit was deep enough to allow him to be introduced slowly. And besides, they were winning, or at least felt like it. They lost their last two games of the road trip, to Golden State in overtime, then to Denver. From there, they won three straight, including a tune-up with New Jersey in which Aguirre scored 31.

That week, the team brought back veteran John Long, the former Piston who had been placed on waivers by Indiana. "The club is close to winning a championship and I want to be part of that," Long said. "I want a ring bad." That alone was reason enough to keep him. McCloskey figured Long as backup insurance at guard, and to

make room, they placed veteran backup center Darryl Dawkins on waivers.

They ended the month on one final sour note. On the morning of February 28, the team learned Salley had fractured his left ankle. Out for at least three weeks, Salley was replaced on the roster by Jim "Robocop" Rowinski, a bruiser out of Purdue who had played in Italy. That night, they were blown out in Cleveland, leaving them five games behind the Cavaliers in the division race. In the second quarter, Mahorn had set a pick that crumpled Cleveland point guard Mark Price. His ensuing concussion would knock Price out of several games and bring a new round of controversy.

As tumultous as February had been, the Pistons finished it 8-3. Times were only going to get better.

MARCH IN A MICROWAVE

Being five games back, the Pistons needed some quick heat as spring

neared. What provides quicker heat than Mr. Microwave? A solid Utah team had come to the Palace, but Vinnie zapped them on high in the second quarter, scoring a team-record 19 consecutive points. He finished the game with 34, and Detroit finished the Jazz, 96-85.

"He was hot, so we kept calling his number," Daly said of Johnson.

"My mechanics were good," Johnson explained. "I felt I was getting a good release."

The burst of heat ignited the Pistons on one of the more stunning turnarounds in modern sports. Over the next two weeks, they would catch, then pass the Cavaliers in the standings on their way to an incredible month.

Two nights later, they took on the Cavs, who were playing without Price, in the Palace. Cleveland had screamed in protest about Mahorn's elbow to Price, and the league answered with another $5,000 fine, the largest ever for an elbowing incident. It was the third $5,000 fine the league had levied against

Mahorn, leading the Pistons power forward to charge that the league was biased against the team.

Before the game, Cavs coach Lenny Wilkens had been greeted with a bomb threat. The meeting was a heated confrontation. Daly exploded in protest in the third period, received his second technical and was tossed out by referee Tommy Nunez. From the locker room, Daly later made contact with the team by telephone, a move that would bring a fine from the league.

"I was just trying to find out what was going on," Daly explained later. He left with Cleveland leading, 55-54.

Suhr took over from there. "I had a lot of help from [assistant coach Brendan Malone] and about 23 other people," Suhr joked later. "All of the players helped me. There was a lady in the third row who helped. Rich, the security guard, told me who to bring in and out. And, of course, [trainer] Mike Abdenour knew everything."

Somebody must have known something. Laimbeer picked the right time to put up some of his best numbers, 24 points with 14 rebounds. And in the clutch, Dumars hit the key shots as Detroit won, 96-90. The outcome cut the Cavs' lead to four games.

But Detroit was still seething from Mahorn's latest fine. "It's us against the world," Laimbeer said, indicating a new rise in Pistons paranoia. Jack McCloskey cautioned his players and urged them to take a more positive approach. Thorn had a job to do, McCloskey said, and although the Detroit general manager thought the league should look just as closely at other teams, he didn't want to make an issue of it. The Pistons played physical basketball, and the officials had to do their job, McCloskey said.

So the players turned their anger to motivation. Mahorn returned to action with 19 rebounds against Denver, just one of numerous yeoman performances by the team's veterans as the Pistons ripped off a run of wins. Miami fell first, as Thomas and Vinnie scored 22 each. Dumars rang up 25 against Denver. Thomas had 27 against Seattle and 34 against Philadelphia, games in which Laimbeer had 19 and 16 rebounds.

"I'm excited by what I'm seeing right now," Thomas said. "We seem to be getting out on the fast break more."

After the Seattle game, Daly was ecstatic. "I really liked our attitude," he said. "We were alive and sharp. That first half may have been one of the best we've played all season."

Against Washington March 12, Laimbeer had 24 points and 16 rebounds. "I see more signs of unselfishness," Daly said later. "We're definitely more cohesive offensively. We're moving the ball more quickly, making that extra pass."

The translation, of course, was that Aguirre had speeded up the offense. It was something the players noticed almost immediately. Thomas, who had never really played organized basketball with Aguirre before, was as surprised as the rest. Rather than waiting for Dantley to work his unique offensive style, the Pistons found themselves benefitting from Aguirre's passing. Eager to fit in, the 6'6" forward was the offensive threat Detroit needed inside to force the double team. As soon as the double arrived, he dumped off the ball, and

Dantley and Isiah shared private words.

the Pistons' perimeter game did the rest.

"We're going in as a unit," Aguirre said proudly. "And to go in as a unit, you're a lot stronger." NBA beat writers began exchanging puzzled glances. Is this the same Mark Aguirre we knew from Dallas?

"Yes," Aguirre said, smiling. "I just shoot less."

In the past, he had been an overwhelmingly confident player, whose confidence fed off his scoring. But since coming to Detroit, he had found other delicacies on which his confidence could dine. "I'm thinking about defense, rebounding, a number of things I have to think about now," he said. "That's the way this team

"They're probably playing the best ball in the league. I'd hate to have to run up against them in the playoffs."

—Hawks coach Mike Fratello

functions and that's the way I want to play."

On March 14, Dumars came out of a mild slump, scoring 30 at Indiana, as they won their eighth straight game, just enough to edge them past the Cavaliers by seven percentage points in the standings. The remarkable turnaround had been accomplished in just two weeks. Thomas was named the NBA Player of the Week for his role in the effort.

Even with the upturn, the money meter followed the Pistons. Edwards and Indiana center Stuart Gray had scuffled late in the game, a move that would bring each of them a $3,500 fine a few days later.

They beat Boston three nights later in the Palace as Vinnie scored 30 and Laimbeer and Rodman controlled the boards. "It was vintage Vinnie," Boston coach Jimmy Rodgers said of the Microman. The Pistons won despite a flatness in their emotions.

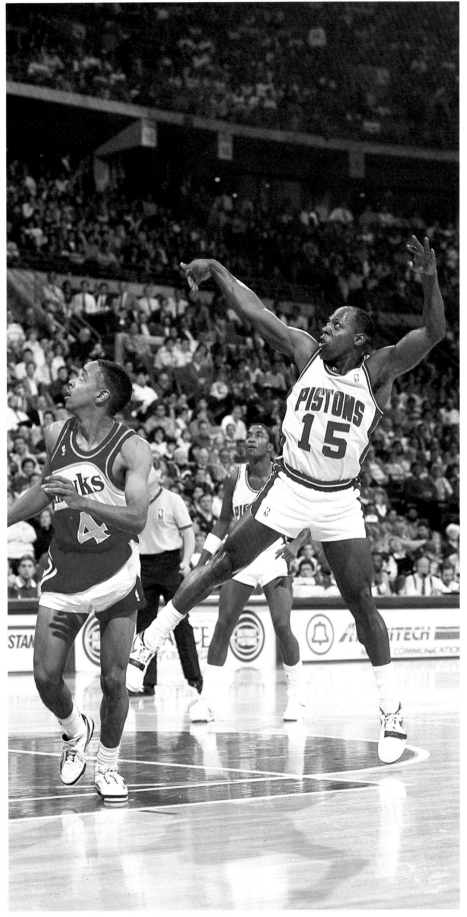

Vinnie heated up the spring. (Einstein photo)

43

Johnson's spark had been enough.

As a little lesson in imperfection, the Bucks whipped 'em in Milwaukee the next night, 117-100. But it would be their only loss of the month. They battered Atlanta in the Omni three nights later in a game that left Hawks coach Mike Fratello gasping. "They're probably playing the best ball in the league," he said. "I'd hate to have to run up against them in the playoffs."

Daly, however, wasn't so sure. "We haven't been playing well," he said, projecting the Cavs, who had regained the division lead by one game, as the favorites. It was needless worry.

From there, they feasted on San Antonio, New Jersey and Charlotte, before Dantley returned to the Palace with the Mavericks. It had potential to be a tense affair, but Thomas and Dantley spoke cordially before the tip-off, the content of their conversation a matter that Thomas said he'd just as soon keep to himself.

The fans, meanwhile, greeted Dantley with a warm welcome. "It felt good," he said later. "It felt funny. You don't realize how great a team they are until you play them. It was great to get the big ovation from the crowd, but I do have feelings about the way things happened. I'll never forget them."

The Pistons moved on from there to a key West Coast trip, starting it off right with a double-overtime victory at Utah. Then Dumars scored 27 two nights later to subdue Seattle, 111-108 (the Pistons had trailed by 25 in the second half), and the Clippers fell after that. They ended the road swing with a loss at Portland, but nobody was complaining when they returned home 3-1. In the middle, the Pistons had closed out March at 16-1, and Daly was again named Coach of the Month.

They returned to the Palace to beat Chicago, with Michael Jordan playing point guard, then went to the Bulls' place two nights later and came away with another overtime win as Vinnie rang up another 30-point game. The card in Chicago featured the now-famous one-round match between Isiah and Bulls center Bill

Aguirre's passing was a major factor.

Cartwright. The decision went to Bill. He received only a $2,500 fine and a one-game suspension.

Zeke got the $5,000 treatment from the league plus a two-game suspension. But the worst levy came from nature: He broke his left hand, a development that left him struggling to regain his shooting form in the midst of rehabilitation over the closing weeks. He played anyway, and fortunately his mates picked up the slack. But there were plenty of worried moments that a stupid fight

had cost them another shot at the title.

Aguirre starred next with 20 points and 11 rebounds as they subdued Milwaukee in the Palace. Then Laimbeer did his thing with 27 points and 11 rebounds for a win in Washington, bringing their record to 57-19. With seven games left, they were set to blast the club win record.

More important, they faced the Cavs in the Palace next, and Vinnie was once again the man. He scored 31, and Detroit won handily, 107-95. Dumars added 19 points and 11 assists. The game also marked Thomas' return to action with his left hand in a flexible cast. He took two shots and missed both in 13 minutes.

Vinnie, however, had filled in admirably. "I wanted the rock, I got the rock," he said of his shooting. "It was just one of those nights."

In the midst of this success, *Rolling Stone* magazine came out with its May 4 issue, featuring the "Motor City Madmen." Except for Dumars, the Pistons had posed in black leather and biker gear for the magazine, but the players didn't like the contents of the story, which portrayed them as, well, Bad Boys.

They lost in New York, then beat Washington at home, setting up a final meeting with the Cavs in the Richfield Coliseum. At 59-19, with a three-and-a-half-game lead on Cleveland, the Pistons were on the verge of claiming the Central Division regular-season title. A win would deliver it. In the locker room before the game, Dumars and Laimbeer decided to play it loose, to take their shots and have fun.

Laimbeer did the damage early, lacing in a series of his long-range, tippy-toed jumpers, as the Pistons took a 20-3 lead by making 10 of their first 12 shots. Dumars, however, did the major damage, going to his unconscious, automatic shot down the stretch. He set a club record with 24 in the third quarter, and finished with 42 points, 11 assists and no turnovers, as Detroit clinched the division title, 118-102.

The Coliseum crowd had been loud and rude to start the contest but was left dumb by the onslaught of Detroit scoring. As the subs mopped up in the closing minutes of the fourth period, the only sound in the vast building was the slapping of the Pistons' hands as the starters and Isiah left the floor.

"I couldn't be happier," Daly told the crowd of reporters that encircled him outside the locker room. "It's been an outstanding year to now, to pretty much come up with the best record and win the division title in perhaps the toughest division in basketball. And particularly in this

building. They're an outstanding club. But our club tonight had kind of a different attitude than I've ever seen in a big game. Billy and Joe said, 'Hey, let's have fun. Let's just shoot the ball.' And Joe was absolutely incredible, on fire. He could not miss a shot. We got help; Vinnie helped at times and Billy helped. And we got good defense at times. It's the way we've been doing basically all year. We played very good defense."

Thomas had struggled with his

shooting throughout his comeback, but had appeared to make progress. "I think Zeke came back and played his best game," Daly said. "People have been saying to me, how come you're playing him? We can't get him back to competition and competing unless we play him. We don't want to go into next week and say, hey, is he going to be ready for the playoffs?"

Actually, there was little question the Pistons were ready for the playoffs. Particularly Dumars. "I wasn't thinking about anything else other than just getting enough room to get the shot off," he said of his scoring outbreak. "That's all I needed."

Asked what had turned the season around, Daly had a quick answer: "I think the win against Cleveland in Detroit was key. We were struggling; I got ejected. I think that win was a key

win for us and started us on a terrific streak of wins. We've got a determined club."

The coach admitted to being surprised by a 60-win season (the Pistons would finish with a regular-season record of 63-19). "Phenomenal," Daly said. "I never would have believed it could have happened. I thought we'd be in the 50s. I thought it might take 55 to win the division. We did it."

One of the most satisfied was Laimbeer, who with Thomas had helped build the team during the 80s. Asked the difference between this team and its competition, Laimbeer replied, "You have a different mentality of players. You have to have talent to win obviously, but you need the mental players, which a lot of average teams don't have. We have an unusually large number of mentally strong players on this ball club. Make no mistake, we did learn from Boston the last few years about how far mental toughness can carry you. They were the champions of the mental toughness department every year. And they had better talent than we did at the time. We've added some more players, but our mental strength has grown through the past few years."

And the big key to the March turnaround? Laimbeer was asked.

"Mark," he said instantly. "Mark's a big key. He passes the crap out of the basketball. When he's double-teamed he hits the open man and hits him quick. It gives the guy who gets the ball the option to take his time and shoot or to make a move and maneuver and get a shot for somebody else. "

For his part, Aguirre was mostly relieved that the team hadn't folded with his addition. "It's done," he said of the regular-season. "We have about 15 minutes of happy time. Chuck Daly's brought us back and we have to handle the next step now. This is an excellent club for preparation. I've never seen a club prepare itself as good as this club does. That's our next step. We're down, and now we're ready to go to the next one."

MONEY TIME

In their history, the Detroit Pistons had never entered a playoff series as the dominant team in pro basketball. They finished the regular season with 63 wins and 19 losses, the best in the league. Which, of course, meant home-court advantage right through to the promised land.

As the Reverend Jesse Jackson might intone, they were somebody.

For better or for worse, that somebody was the Bad Boys.

All season long, the media had kept a running toll of fines the league levied against the Pistons. But the other side of the coin, so to speak, is that winners do well in the marketplace. Heading into the playoffs, fans had purchased an estimated $3 million worth of Bad Boys paraphernalia.

Those sales were just one facet of the franchise's new financial health.

"You must understand, this club lost money in each of its first 35 seasons. I believe that's the only club record we hold in professional sports."

—Thomas Wilson

Foremost was the gate. The Pistons led the league in the number of season tickets sold, 15,500. Their new $70 million arena, the Palace, had sold its 21,454 seating capacity for every game. Even after salaries, light bills, and all those other operating costs, the Pistons showed a bottom line of about $8 million, reportedly the most lucrative in the team's 40-year history.

"You must understand, this club lost money in each of its first 35 seasons," Thomas Wilson, the Pistons chief executive officer, explained. "I believe that's the only record we hold in professional sports."

Even in the 1980s, there was a time when the Pistons considered it a successful season if they lost only $5 million. In those days, they had trouble getting people's attention.

"It's not that we were a team of bad history," Wilson said. "It's more that we were a team of no history. In a town that was rabid about the Tigers, Lions and Redwings, we were just an afterthought."

Frankly, the Pistons had never won enough to merit much of any kind of thought, fore, after, or otherwise. No other team had been in the league so long without winning a title.

A fellow by the name of Fred

The Palace was a sell-out for every game.

46

By 1989 the Pistons were anything but boring. (Einstein photo)

McCloskey was a key factor in the turnaround.

Zollner had founded the club in 1948 in Fort Wayne, Indiana. He was in the pistons business and named the team for his product, the Fort Wayne Pistons. In 1955 and '56, the Pistons went to the NBA Finals but lost both times. They moved to Detroit in '57 but showed little torque. For the next 25 years, the Pistons didn't even make the playoffs.

In 1974, William Davidson bought them for $8.1 million. Today that figure sounds like a bargain. Back then, it was a big-league gamble. But Davidson was a patient kind of guy, known for taking the time to turn a business around. But even he had to wonder. By 1979, the team's value had shrunk to $5 million. It was obvious changes had to be made. As with all changes, some were good, some bad.

Over the years, the team had filled Cobo Hall with a lot of losing memories but not many fans. So in '78, the Pistons shifted out of urban Detroit to the vast Silverdome, the football stadium in the suburbs with 62,000 seats. Never mind that it was chilly and drafty; the vast emptiness of the building created game atmospheres in those early days that could rival a wake.

Perhaps that's what the team needed, for the Pistons seemed to die in 1979, when they gave M.L. Carr and two first-round draft picks to Boston for Robert McAdoo. Of all Boston's victories over Detroit, that one left the longest sting. The Celtics used their picks to acquire Robert Parish and draft Kevin McHale. Meanwhile, the Pistons finished the season 16-66, then McAdoo got

injured after six games the following year. Eventually, the team released him.

Davidson knows exactly when the dark skies lightened. Draft day 1981, when the Pistons picked Thomas out of Indiana and Notre Dame forward Kelly Tripucka. "That was the precise moment, the day, that things turned around for us," Davidson said. "Suddenly, we had two young, good-looking, talented players. Suddenly, we had a future. Suddenly, people started coming to games."

To create interest in the on-court improvement, the team launched a shameless marketing campaign, the kind that rivaled the best used-car hawking. There were discounts and giveaways galore. "We broke every rule of sports marketing and common decency," Wilson said. "It's embarrassing to look back. But it brought people in and got us noticed by the media. And once we got the people out for free, we figured they might be willing to pay the next time."

Eventually, they were.

It also helped immensely that they hired Jack McCloskey as general manager in 1979. He was the son of a Pennsylvania coal miner and every bit as tough. It took time for this toughness to find its way onto the court; it always does in the NBA. But McCloskey was an unbridled competitor. If you think that last line is a little diversion in hype, you've obviously never played Jack in tennis. He takes sets, even if he has to jump the net and fight you for them. Sometimes, it has been said, he prefers to get them that way. He was a two-time MVP of the old Eastern League, the one-time farm circuit of the NBA, where the players all held day jobs and rough-housed as semi-pros on the weekend. You could say they did it for the love of the game, except it was rougher than that. McCloskey was a Pennsylvania high school coach in those days. To give you an idea of his competitiveness, he once went into a shower and choked a startled ref because of a late-game call that cost him a win. The influence of a well-connected friend got him out of that one, and

As was Isiah.

McCloskey worked his way through a distinguished coaching career in college and the pros. The Pistons had been wimps far too long when he arrived there in 1979. It was an image that departed with his arrival.

In addition to his fearless maneuvering of personnel, McCloskey made another of those key moves in building the Pistons. He hired Chuck Daly as coach in 1983. Where Tripucka and Thomas were young and handsome, Daly was well into his 50s and had a game face that resembled Leonid Breshnev. But he had an eye for sartorial splendor and a heart of old-fashioned basketball values. Another Pennsylvania boy, he loved defense and team principles. Daly became the persona "Daddy Rich," a charming gentleman with a hard-boiled glare that belied his patience.

Between McCloskey and Daly and Thomas, they became pretty good. On the court and at the box office.

The rivalry with the Boston Celtics grew to the point that 61,983 fans filled the Silverdome for a regular-season meeting in 1987-88. The Pistons set an NBA attendance record that season, one that probably won't be equalled. It came on the heels of the Pistons' distinction as the first team in NBA history to draw one million fans in a season.

But all those people made the Silverdome about as cozy as it was gonna get. It simply wasn't a basketball facility. With the need for a Pistons arena obvious, Davidson and a group of partners acquired land in Auburn Hills, northwest of Detroit, and built the Palace.

It's quite a place. State-of-the-art, the *Philadelphia Inquirer* called it. The floor is ringed by 180 luxury suites, some of which rent for as much as $120,000 per year. The rent of those boxes gave the owners a chunk of change to knock down the debt service not long after the building opened. As with any new building, the atmosphere required an adjustment. But the fans soon settled in and found something to get loud about.

If nothing else, it seems, the Bad Boys had picked up the tab on a lot of Bad Years.

For those reasons, the sense of momentum went beyond mere basketball in the spring of 1989. Hopes were high heading into the playoffs that the Pistons could do something they had never done before.

BRUSH OF THE BROOM

Actually it was a pretender who started this broom motif in the 1989 NBA playoffs. The Knicks swept the Philadelphia 76ers in three close first-round games, and in a fit of youthful excess, the New York players grabbed brooms from the custodial staff in Philadelphia and began doing the floor. It was a hoot. At least it seemed that way until Chicago upset New York in the next round of the playoffs. Perhaps then the Knicks realized they had been grossly cocky.

For better or worse, the tone had been set for the "second season." Detroit made a sweep of the first two rounds of the playoffs, and the Los Angeles Lakers blasted to the Finals by winning 11 straight games. Any hopes the TV people had for a little drama went right out the door with the dust. Michael Jordan and the Bulls provided about the only element of suspense, but that's getting a bit ahead of the story.

For the Pistons, the first sweet brush of the broom came in round one against the Celtics. Playing without Larry Bird, Boston had struggled to make the eighth playoff spot in the Eastern Conference. But the Celtics came to Detroit determined to get a win. Even without Bird, Boston still had perhaps the best frontcourt offense in the business, featuring McHale and Parish.

But it took the Pistons less than one half of basketball to establish their supremacy. They did it with an impressive display of interior defense in the second quarter of game one. The perpetrators of this defense were John Salley and Dennis Rodman. By then, Rodman's story was old hat. Everybody knew he was going to play defense and rebound as if those were the only two services on the planet. Salley, on the other, had become a seven-foot question mark by the end of the season. Would he be traded? Would he get to play?

Injuries had dogged him all season, but the low point of the year came as he was perfectly healthy, as the rest of the team was flying high. On April 18, when the Pistons dashed Cleveland for the Central title, Salley played but a few seconds of garbage time. Afterward, while his teammates basked in their accomplishment, Salley made a quick exit of the locker room. He knew the lack of playing time had been another message from Daly that the team was displeased with him.

Thomas became the interpreter of these communications in a talk with Salley later that night. "We had a long talk that I needed," Salley said. "A lot of guys had stepped up their focus when I got hurt and I needed to. He told me I needed to be more focused... Isiah is straightforward. He told me, 'Look, you're a great guy and all that, but bleep that. We need you

The Celts felt a bit blue in the Palace. (Einstein photo)

for hoops.' He said, 'I've got a broken hand, and I'm playing.'

Actually, it was a message that had been sent before. "I've said all along, if Salley becomes the type of basketball player that we all think he can be, this will be a great basketball team," Thomas said when asked about Salley. "This can be a team that can be compared to the Celtics, the Lakers and those teams of the past. If he becomes the type of basketball player that elevates our level. It makes us a great basketball

team, as compared to a very, very good basketball team."

John Salley made them a great basketball team that first game against the Celtics. He and Rodman blocked seven shots between them in the second quarter alone, turning the game into a nightmare from which Boston never woke up. The Celtics scored just 10 points in the second period, tying an all-time NBA playoff low. That combined with 16 points by Dumars in the first half allowed the Pistons to breeze, 101-91. Salley

Rodman had helped the Pistons overcome the Boston Garden atmosphere. (Steve Lipofsky photo)

finished with 15 points, seven rebounds, six blocked shots, and two assists.

What did you feed Salley today? reporters asked Chuck Daly afterward.

"I don't know," he said, "but it's the best game he has played this year since the seventh game last year against the Lakers. I don't know why it comes and where it goes, but he was sensational. Shot blocking, offensive-minded, aggressive. We ought to bottle it and find out what it was."

Rodman had been just as potent, especially when the Pistons moved their tempo up a notch at the close of the first quarter. "That's his kind of game," Daly said of Rodman. "He gets going offensively, gets second shots, rebounds, runs out."

Laimbeer finished with 12 rebounds, and when the Celtics opened the game by playing a guard against him, the Pistons center moved his offense inside and scored on a variety of surprisingly athletic moves. "I can score," Laimbeer replied when reporters asked about his display of athleticism. "I have confidence in myself. It's just our team offense is not oriented for me to be in the post. We have a lot of offensive weapons. A lot of people can score from different areas on the court. If they continue to put a small guy on me, I'll have to continue to go inside like I did tonight."

Daly said he was just glad that someone had come through, particularly in the early going when the Pistons' guards couldn't seem to score. "Vinnie struggled. Zeke struggled," Daly said. "We looked like we had three days off. We had good intensity but we didn't look real sharp, either individually or execution-wise."

For Salley, the troubles couldn't have ended sooner. Rather than hustling out of the locker room, he decided to hang around and talk about the night with reporters. "I'm very happy," he said as he finally packed up his bag to leave. "I want to go home, sit in my jacuzzi and probably talk to my mother and father and go to sleep. And try to forget it

and just come back with the same attitude on Sunday."

He returned with his newfound intensity Sunday, but the Celtics stepped their game up a notch, too. Well into the third period, Boston held a nine-point lead. But again Daly went to Rodman and Salley, and again their defense delivered. As they tightened up on the Celtics' offense, Thomas celebrated his 28th birthday with a 14-point third quarter. For the game, he scored 26, the first real outburst since his hand injury.

The fourth period, meanwhile, belonged to Detroit's defense. They held the Celtics to 13 points and claimed their second win of the series, 102-95.

That pattern repeated itself two

"I'm very happy. I want to go home, sit in my jacuzzi and probably talk to my mother and father and go to sleep. And try to come back with the same attitude on Sunday."

—John Salley

nights later in Boston Garden. This time, Vinnie scored 25 and Dumars 24 to carry the offensive load. And again, the interior defense was led by Salley, who played 30 minutes and was a large factor in keeping Boston away from its dominant inside game.

"They had the answers for everything," Boston coach Jimmy Rodgers said afterward.

Somebody asked Dumars about Detroit being a team of destiny. "I don't know about destiny," he replied. "I just believe in hard work. Period."

You'd have a hard time convincing the Milwaukee Bucks about the destiny thing, though. They engaged in a first-round battle with Atlanta and entered the Eastern Conference semifinals with Paul Pressey and Terry Cummings out with injuries.

From there, the situation only worsened.

Detroit, meanwhile, had an eight-day layoff while waiting for the Bucks and Hawks to settle their bout. When Milwaukee finally advanced, the Pistons found themselves a bit rusty.

Milwaukee came to Detroit fresh from Atlanta and immediately turned their intensity loose. Midway through the second period, the Bucks led by 13. The Pistons accommodated them by shooting a mere 38 percent from the floor. True to their pattern, the Pistons' defense was the security blanket, holding the Bucks to only 32 points in the second half, 11 in the fourth quarter. Which was enough for an 85-80 win. On offense, Laimbeer was the lead factor with 19 points and 17 rebounds, and Salley scored 14, many of them during the turnaround.

The injury situation worsened for the Bucks before game two, when backup center Paul Mokeski was lost. Still, they battled the Pistons to a tie at the half, but by the end of the third, Detroit led by 7, enough for their defense to do the rest. Salley turned on the offensive burners with 15 points in the fourth (he finished with 23), as the Pistons claimed game two 112-92.

Game three got worse for the Bucks when forward Larry Krystkowiak suffered a severe knee injury in the first minute of play. The crowd and Bucks coach Del Harris screamed for a foul on Laimbeer, but replays of the incident showed Krystkowiak's knee buckled as he broke to the basket. As he was being wheeled from the court on a stretcher, Krystkowiak offered one last expression of spirit, raising his fist. The crowd responded loudly, but the Bucks had felt the wind knocked out of them. They trailed the whole game, and it got worse in the third period, when Daly moved Thomas to shooting guard and put Dumars at the point. Free to work on his scoring, Thomas knocked down 15 points in the third on his way to a 26-point night. The Pistons offense seemed to be clicking again, with six people in double figures. They moved up 3-0 in the series with a 110-90 win.

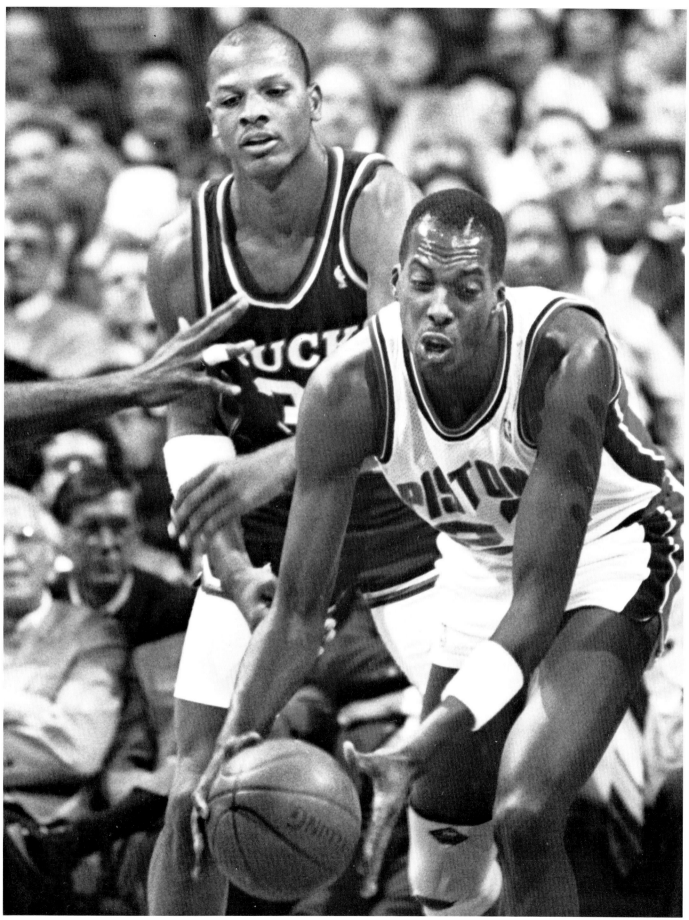

Spider became a terror in the playoffs.

Laimbeer played well against the Bucks.

Out West, the Lakers had finished off Seattle, 4-0, creating an atmosphere of sweep across the league. Nowhere was this feeling more prevalent than in Milwaukee, where the Bucks faced game four with a seven-man roster. Milwaukee responded with spirit and jumped out to a 21-point lead in the first half. Fortunately, the Pistons' offense was still clicking. And for a change, the five starters carried the responsibility. All five finished in double-figure scoring, with Dumars leading the way at 22. They shot 56 percent from the field, pulled within 10 by halftime, and led by five heading into the fourth period. With no reserves, tired legs did the Bucks in as much as Detroit did. It never did get easy, however. The Bad Boys walked, 96-94, after

Milwaukee failed at a last-second attempt to overcome a three-point deficit.

"Defense was the constant throughout the series," Dumars said afterward. "The shots didn't fall always, the break wasn't always there, we missed some free throws, but defense was there always."

So was the luck, Thomas added. Not only were the Bucks injured, they didn't shoot well.

For Thomas, the best news was that he had the full range of motion back to his hand. "I can squeeze it," he said. "I can hold the basketball now. I can dribble the basketball. I can take my regular shot now as opposed to taking a different shot. It started feeling better during the layoff. It is a great relief because, I wasn't

able to play at Isiah's standards. I'm just glad my teammates and the fans were patient enough to let me keep playing and get this thing together."

Yet the ups and downs with his shooting were far from over. Just when he thought he had adjusted, Michael Jordan entered the picture, and things got shaky all over again.

ZEKE'S VISION

The wielder of the broom always faces the problem of a clean house. Having dusted Boston and Milwaukee, the Pistons found themselves with nothing to do but wait until Chicago and New York settled their series.

Faced with a layoff, Chuck Daly sat home the morning after the Milwaukee series trying to figure how to keep the Bad Boys sharp, focused, engaged, championship-ready. Basketball is a game of timing, and to keep it, players have to play.

Daly's mind turned to his good friend, Billy Cunningham, who had coached the Philadelphia 76ers through a sweeping route to the 1983 NBA title. Like the Pistons of '89, the '76ers faced long layoffs between series. Just as Daly was thinking about this problem, Cunningham happened to phone to inquire about another matter. So while Daly had the former Philadelphia coach on the line, he popped the question. Just what did you do to keep your guys fresh during the layoffs?

"He said, 'I don't think it matters as long as your team understands where they want to go and what they want to do,' " Daly said later. "Billy Cunningham said if a team has the concentration and the motivation, they will handle it."

That, in itself, helped put Daly's mind at ease. His was a focused basketball team. Mahorn, Laimbeer, Johnson, Dumars, all of them wanted this thing badly.

And then there was Isiah Thomas.

The others really desired to be champions, but Zeke seemed entranced by the notion. Passion. Insanity. Blind pursuit. All the romance-fiction terms applied. He had spent his NBA career studying the people who won world championships, particularly his friend, Magic Johnson. Thomas wanted to know what they knew. For whatever reasons, he had turned this study into a mystical quest. He revered winners. Bird. Magic. Pat Riley. K.C. Jones. He wanted to be one. Like them. A winner. He flattered them. Cajoled them. He wanted to duplicate them in Detroit. Whatever he could steal, he stole. The mannerisms were the easy part. Getting inside their minds was the real challenge. He wanted to think like an NBA champion.

He would pick Magic's brain in late-night phone calls to the West Coast. "I hate that I taught him," Magic would say later. "That's the only thing. I should go back and kick myself."

For the most part, it was only knowledge. The real wisdom Isiah would have to earn himself. The hard way. Every time it seemed he had it down, some other unseen factor would get in the way. Detroit battled Boston in the '87 Eastern finals, but the Celtics escaped on Isiah's mental error in game five. The last big lesson had come from Magic in the 1988 Finals.

At last, the 1989 season seemed the time. To it, Thomas brought everything he had learned from his years of study.Over time, he had come to understand that ilt wasn't an athletic pursuit, for the most part. It was mental. Serious mental. Watching him go through it, you were impressed by the fact that by his eighth season in the league, Isiah Thomas knew exactly what he was doing.

He knew because he had visualized it, mixed the facts he had accumulated with his imagination to create a model of his ultimate success. Looking at it like that, it's easy to understand why the Pistons didn't win the title in 1988. Isiah simply didn't have the complete vision. But the loss to the Lakers in '88 had forced him to add more definition, more items of detail to his dream. In putting it together, he settled for nothing less than purity. He

Aguirre helped out with the scoring.

wanted to win every playoff game on the way to sweeping the title.

It was grandiose, and he didn't tell people about it, not the sweep part anyway. In reality, he would settle for the title any old way he could get it. Hook. Crook. Murder. Whatever. But his dream was one big sweep, 15 games without a loss.

The clearer the picture he had of it, the easier it was for him to explain the vision to other people. John Salley was a mere sub, yet Thomas knew his role was important. So Thomas went to Salley and told him what to do. Salley was part of the dream. As were all of the rest. As Joe Dumars explained, the vision was originally Isiah's, but he spent his time convincing everybody else. And soon it was their dream, too. They all could see it, could see that he was dying to get it.

Why did he want it so badly? Some observers have theorized that his drive came from his meager beginnings in a Chicago ghetto. Many kids have come out of the ghetto playing basketball, yet few have driven themselves to the point of exhaustion to win a championship. Thomas had brought the same type of desire to the University of Indiana, where as a sophomore he led the Hoosiers to the NCAA championship.

He really didn't have to prove anything when he got to the Pistons. He was a bright young guard who showed he was a brilliant offensive performer. But he was only 6'1". Nobody really expected him to be dominant. He could have had a lot of fun and made great money just being Isiah. But he wanted to be more than Isiah. He wanted to be bathed in that ineffable light of joy reserved for champions.

Boston Celtics President Red Auerbach has a theory about truly great players that he has seen proven time and time again: The more money you give them, the harder they work to prove they're worth it. "That's true of the Larry Birds and Magic Johnsons," Auerbach said.

Thomas badly wanted to be considered the equal of Johnson and Bird. After the loss in the 1988 Finals,

Thomas demanded that the Pistons renegotiate his contract, upward from the $750,000 per year he was making to $2 million per season, close to what other superstars made. The negotiations were a bit thorny through the summer, but finally in the fall the team gave Thomas the contract he wanted. And then he set out to prove he was worth it. Perhaps Auerbach's theory went to work from there. Thomas had an even greater incentive to reach his goal.

Not that he really needed any

more incentive. He was already consumed by it.

After the win over Boston in the '88 Eastern finals, Isiah re-examined the details, looking for the reasons he had succeeded. He decided winning was a function of mind over matter. He became intrigued with a definition of fantasy—when your dreams meet reality. For him, the process became a matter of forcing your dreams into real life. Once he had it set like that in his mind, it became "do-able," as they say in the business vernacular.

Thomas had dreams of a title.

56

All of which explains why Thomas became so upset with himself over the stupid fight with Cartwright late in the season. He had come dangerously close to shattering his dream. Wasted opportunities like that can break people. And because he wanted this championship so badly, Isiah Thomas was very capable of being broken.

SWEET HOME CHICAGO

Finally, Chicago downed New York and advanced to the Eastern Conference finals. That seemed good because Chicago hadn't beaten Detroit all season. On the other hand, New York had been very successful against the Pistons. But Isiah would have preferred to play the Knicks. He was concerned about the Bulls. Mike Jordan was on an almost supernatural roll, having come up with brilliant performances to defeat Cleveland and New York. Chicago presented bad vibes for Isiah's vision.

By the eve of game one of the Eastern Conference finals, Isiah felt he had worked his shooting form back into shape. No longer did he feel hampered by his broken left hand. The night before the Chicago series opened his shot seemed unstoppable as he worked in the gym at his home, drilling an incredible run of long-range jumpers. He knew he was getting the strength back in his hand.

But that Sunday afternoon, the shot that had seemed so sure the night before turned strange again. "I didn't have a feel for the ball all night," he would say afterward. "Even on my free throws I didn't feel comfortable."

Chicago had something to do with it. The Bulls came out with Jordan playing Thomas. The Chicago star had moved to point guard late in the spring, but this was the first time that Isiah had become his defensive assignment for an entire game. Jordan's height and leaping ability provided something of a distraction on the perimeter. But that wasn't the real problem. Isiah simply couldn't hit the shot. Not that he didn't shoot. But the ball kept rimming out.

As a result, Jordan backed off and let him shoot even more. If he had hit a few shots, Jordan would have been forced to come out further and play him. Then Isiah could have driven by him, or pushed the ball inside to Aguirre. But missing from the perimeter left an impossible situation.

Thomas made only three of 18 shots on the afternoon.

"Anytime that he would drive I was anticipating that," Jordan said afterward. "I wanted to make him shoot the outside shot, and he didn't hit that today. That's not to say I did an outstanding defensive job."

To compound the situation, neither Joe nor Vinnie was hitting either. Detroit fell behind by 24 in the second quarter, which was reason

Winning was a function of mind over matter.

Edwards operates against Chicago.

for concern. But the Pistons had come back so many times in the past, no one in the Palace crowd seemed ready to panic.

Sure enough, they came back, taking the lead midway through the fourth period. But they never did get straightened out offensively. Some days you hit the shots, some days you don't. On that Sunday, the Bad Boys didn't. The Bulls did, and just like that, they took the game, 94-88, and a 1-0 lead in the series. The homecourt advantage the Pistons had worked so hard for all year was gone in an afternoon.

"It is going to be hard to catch them on their heels like we caught them today," Jordan told reporters. "But we have a good chance to win the series."

Asked how the Bulls withstood Detroit's comeback, Chicago coach Doug Collins replied, "I just basically told our guys to try to maintain your poise as much as you possibly can. Detroit is the best defensive team in the league, and when they come at you you know you have to make sure you get a good shot. I just told our guys to lay it on the line. We are here, the ball's loose on the floor, you have got to get it."

How surprised are you? the writers asked Collins.

"I am very surprised and you are too," he said.

Chuck Daly wasn't all that surprised. The outcome was just what he had worried about. "They did exactly what they did in the previous two series," he said. "We gave up 28 points on second shots, which was an overall disaster. And we missed 10 free throws down the stretch. Obviously, I didn't do a good job with the layoff. So, I've got to accept the responsibility. Our guards were something like 11 for 46."

In the Detroit locker room, the reporters were packed shoulder-to-shoulder. It was difficult to move. Thomas remained in the showers longer than usual. The longer he stayed, the larger the crowd of reporters waiting to interview him grew. Finally, he emerged, worked through the crowd, and sat, his back

to the wall, facing the ring of cameras, lights, and microphones.

Just as the questions began flying, Aguirre parted the crowd and bent near Isiah to borrow some lotion from a large dispenser. "Are we having grits tonight?" Aguirre asked, laughing, trying to break his friend's obvious depression.

Thomas gave a sickly smile and turned his attention to the throng. One after another, in a calm, measured tone, he answered all of the questions, patiently discussing every notion they could think of. Each time, he came to a very simple

> **"They gave our guards the shot, and we couldn't put the ball in the hole. And that took our inside game away. Normally we pray and beg for shots like we were getting. We were just standing there open."**
>
> **—Isiah Thomas**

answer: "We didn't hit the shots."

Was there a feeling that you were going to be invincible? one writer asked.

"No," he said, "we never belived we were invinciable. I think had Milwaukee been a healthy team, they would have beaten us a couple of games."

The questions went on for 45 minutes, until the locker room was nearly empty, except for New York Post writer Peter Vecsey, who lingered, trying to extract something extra. What really happened? Vescey asked Thomas.

"All night long I was searching for someone to get hot," Isiah said. "Aguirre got hot, but they started dropping off on him. They gave our guards the shot, and we couldn't put the ball in the hole. And that took our inside game away. Normally we pray and beg for shots like we were getting.

We were just standing there open."

Thomas finished tying his necktie and sighed heavily. He looked sick.

"This is a strange game sometimes," he said.

He grabbed his gym bag and headed for the door. As he hit the hallway, Mike Ornstein, a friend from Los Angeles, stepped up and took the bag. "Let me carry this for you," Ornstein said and slapped Thomas on the back.

They rode around aimlessly for several hours after that, Ornstein said later, and Thomas never said a word.

In the press room, columnist Shelby Strother of the Detroit News summed up the situation. "He just might die of natural causes," he said of Thomas.

There was, however, no need for obituaries two nights later. Zeke found his shot, or at least a good part of it. He scored 33 and Dumars 20 to carry the Pistons to a 100-91 win, evening the series at one all.

From there, it moved to ancient Chicago Stadium, where the Pistons came out strong on Aguirre's offense. They quieted the crowd, and with seven minutes left held a 14-point lead. But just as the fourth quarter seemed like Bad Boy time again, they blinked, Jordan winked, and the game went down to a final sequence.

The Bulls had charged back to tie it at 97, leaving the Pistons with possession and 0:28 on the clock. Isiah worked the ball on the perimeter, and at about 0:10 Laimbeer came out to set his usual pick, allowing Isiah to veer right for the shot, or perhaps to flip it back to Laimbeer for one of his tippy-toes deals. But in setting the pick, Laimbeer shifted and bowed his leg enough to catch Jordan. Offensive foul. And it was a correct call, although the circumstances were tough. Jordan, of course, took the ball at the other end, as he had done so many times before, and put the shot down, giving Chicago a 99-97 win and a 2-1 lead in the series.

Jordan had scored 46 points, the first real time in the series that he had put together a solid offensive game. The Pistons knew they couldn't let it

Laimbeer did his boardwork.

Jordan's winning shot in Game 3.

happen again. So they decided to make Jordan play point guard like a real point guard. They double-teamed him and forced him to pass the ball. Jordan was too great a player to take a bad shot. He would rather give the ball to a teammate. And the Pistons weren't about to let the other Bulls beat them.

"When he puts his mind to it, you can't stop him," Thomas said of Jordan. "That's the whole key. We're hoping you can take his mind off of it."

The shutdown worked. As usual, Dumars had the primary responsibility with Jordan. But Vinnie and Isiah both took their turns. And Rodman helped out. Boy, did he help out. Jordan was five for 15 in game four. As a team, the Bulls shot 39 percent from the floor. The Pistons shot 36 percent. It didn't matter. Thomas scored 27, and the defense was the real difference as they won 86-80 and tied the series at two all.

Back at the Palace for game five, the Pistons did an even better job against Jordan, holding him to just eight shots from the floor (he made four) and 18 points. Meanwhile, the Pistons offense was balanced, with Vinnie getting 22, Aguirre 19, Thomas 17 and James Edwards 12. Rodman turned in one of his superfreak games with 14 rebounds, 0 points and will-breaking defense. All combined, it totalled a 94-85 win and a 3-2 series lead for the Bad Boys.

The Chicago crowd was loud and proud for game six back at the Stadium. They got louder early in the first period when small forward Scottie Pippen suffered a concussion trying to crash the boards for an offensive rebound. Collins and the crowd claimed Laimbeer's elbow was the perpetrator. Replays showed the contact was clearly inadvertent, and there was no foul. Pippen, however, went to the hospital for observation. And Zeke went on to another big

night, particularly after he moved to shooting guard and Dumars to the point. Thomas scored 33 points, many of them down the stretch as Chicago faltered. Jordan matched it with 32, but that wasn't enough. Dennis Rodman turned in another hyper defensive effort, and Detroit prevailed again, 103-94, to end the series.

As Jordan headed toward the bench in the final seconds, he paused to speak with Dumars. "He came by," Joe said later, "and shook my hand and said, 'Bring it back to the East.' I said, 'I don't miss you, Mike. See you next year.' There's always a fear that giving your most, giving your best, may not be enough with him. You have to raise your level. You're playing against somebody like him, there's no holding back."

Once again, the Bad Boys were headed to the Finals.

In the press interview area, a throng of reporters gathered, one of them being a blind radio man with some kind of microphone attached to a booming sound system. The blind guy wore no sunglasses over his pale, hooded eyes. With his sound system dominated the proceedings, he asked concise, pointed questions. As Isiah stepped to the podium, the blind man boomed the first one out.

"Isiah," he asked, "could you talk about getting another chance in the championship series at the Lakers. What does that mean to you now?"

"It means a lot," Thomas replied. "I understand now what the Celtics and the Lakers have gone through for all those years. When we lost the last games of the NBA Finals last year, we decided we were going to have the best record in the NBA, we're going to get to the Finals and we're going to win it. Well, we've done two of the three, and I wanted to tell you that it is a hard, hard job. And I've got a tremendous amount of respect for the Lakers and the Celtics because this is our second year in a row of being in the Finals and I know how difficult a process it is. So that says a lot about the individual people who were playing on those teams."

After another half dozen questions, Isiah stepped down from the podium and headed down the hallway toward the locker room, a group of young fans trailing after him. Outside the locker room, he stopped for hugs and kisses from his family. As he entered, he encountered Hubie Brown, the CBS analyst and former Knicks coach who grabbed him in a full embrace. Upon his entrance to the locker room, the faces there all turned to him, followed by shouts of "Zeke." It seemed that everyone at once reached for his hand. He grinned and rose up on his toes to look out across the crowd. "I'm done," he said, beaming. "It's somebody else's job to get the championship." Among the first to greet him was Dick Stockton, the CBS play-by-play man who told him not to kiss Magic so much in this year's Finals.

"I'm gonna bite him," Isiah said.

Everybody laughed.

Quickly the reporters found him and circled in again. How sweet is

Mahorn works the Bulls inside.

this? one of them asked.

"It's nice to be in the Finals," Thomas said, "but it's a little different this time because we're just not satisfied with getting into the Finals. I know it's nice, we're going to celebrate, we're going to relish the accomplishment, but it just started. It's nowhere near over.

"When we came back into training camp this year, we just wished we could have not even had a regular season. We just wanted the playoffs to begin so we could get right back into the Finals. But instead we had to go through all of this."

"The Bad Boys," another reporter said, "were having a little fun with you afterward, saying, 'We see you finally came through for us. That's what you're getting the big bucks for, you should be doing that more often.' How did it feel just to take control down the stretch and seal it?"

"Rodman made some great plays,"

Thomas replied. "If anybody took control—you know you look at the points and Isiah scored some points—but Rodman took control."

Actually, he added, the entire team had played well. "We got some good offense by James, Joe, Vinnie, myself, Mark," Isiah said, "and we put together a good half of offensive basketball with a good game of excellent defense."

As the media crowd thinned out, filmmaker Spike Lee made his rounds through the locker room, pausing in front of Isiah's cubicle to snap a few shots with a small automatic flash camera.

"Spike!" Isiah said. "How ya doin'? I saw you on TV this morning."

Lee, the Mars Blackmon in Nike's Air Jordan commercials, smiled and shook Isiah's hand lightly, which was a surprise because Isiah hadn't been shaking hands. Later another

well-wisher offered to shake.

"My hand's all messed up," he said with a laugh. Salley had inadvertently stepped on it during an outbreak of cheering on the Detroit bench. Besides his hand, Thomas ached from a hamstring pull suffered late in the second quarter. All these things, however, would be put aside. The Lakers were just down the road, and Zeke was not about to be denied.

The dream had suffered some dents against Chicago, but it had survived. "I wanted a shot at Philadelphia's 11-1 record," Isiah said of the 76ers' performance in the 1983 playoffs.

Dressed in white Giorgio deck shoes and a white captain's hat, Thomas walked out smiling. All that was left in the locker room were souvenir hunters looking for something special. But the Pistons had already taken it and gone.

Jordan had given the bench reason for concern. (Einstein photo)

THE SEQUEL

The Detroit papers had fun with the Pistons/Lakers rematch in the Finals, calling it "The Sequel." As things turned out, it had the properties of a sequel. Big on staging, hype and promotion. Plenty of talent. A bit short on dramatic sequences. But, hey, that was okay for the Motown crowd. Like we said at the top of the show, for the Pistons, drama was a disease. They wanted the trophy with as few complications as possible.

"In training camp," Laimbeer said, "we knew that we wanted to get back to the finals, we wanted to win a championship. And we set about a game plan where we had to do A, B, C and D to get back there. We've done A, B, C and D. Now comes the E part."

Heading into the series, "the E part" seemed to stand for effort, excellence, earnest, Earvin, enigmatic, euphoric, Edwards. Anything but easy.

After all, the Pistons were facing Magic Johnson, who had a real shot at three-peating, the L.A. term for staking out a plot of basketball history by claiming three consecutive titles. The Home Boys knew Earvin wanted a piece of that action. It was what he lived for. Besides, 42-year-old Kareem Abdul-Jabbar would be retiring after the season, his 20th in the NBA. The Cap wanted to end things with another ring.

With all this incentive, the Lakers had founded their own little broom cult, brushing their way along an 11-0 run to the Finals. Seattle, Golden State, Phoenix—each had gone out with the dustpan. To a man, the Pistons knew Magic and company would be dangerous. No one knew it better than Thomas. Whenever he spoke of them, his voice tried to cloak his concern in respect.

"I undertand the Lakers as a basketball team," he said. "But more importantly, I understand them as people. In order to beat the opponent you got to understand the people that you're playing against. Because in a playoff, plays don't beat you, passing and all that. What beats you in the playoffs is people, individual people digging deep down within themselves and deciding that they're going to win a basketball game. That's what beats you."

Translation: Look out for Earvin. He'll find a way to win.

This respect, however, didn't translate into a newfound meekness. They were still the Bad Boys. "L.A. has our rings from last year and we want our own ring," Laimbeer said. "And that's enough incentive right there."

At the outset, the potential for drama seemed high. It wasn't hard to imagine the Lakers stealing a third title and the Bad Boys condemned to a life as Bridesmaids in Hell. The worries—not to mention the dramatic possibilities—began to soften before Game One in Detroit, when the Lakers Byron Scott suffered a severe hamstring injury. He would miss at least the first two games, the injury report said.

The Pistons immediately pointed out that they weren't big on sympathy cards, however. After all, it's not hard to argue that if Mahorn and Thomas hadn't been injured during the 1988 Finals, the Bad Boys could have claimed the prize right then.

What did the loss of Scott mean to the Lakers? a writer asked Isiah. "I don't know what it means to them and I don't care," Thomas said quickly.

The Finals were Kareem's last hurrah.

"They didn't care about me last year when I was hurt."

The Pistons further emphasized this lack of human compassion by absolutely smoking the Lakers in Game One. They did it the old-fashioned way, too, with the guards popping from every place on the floor. For the record, Zeke did 24, Joe 22, and the Microman 19. Nobody was happier to see the Boys back than Daly. During the Chicago series, the backcourt had shot less than 40 percent from the field, a development that had him looking more and more like Leonid Brezhnev in the huddle during timeouts. When things were going bad, Daly would sort of dip his chin, tilting his gaze up through his bushy eyebrows. Very glum.

But there was none of that in Game One against the Lakers. With six minutes left in the game, Detroit led, 97-79. After the late patty-cakes, they finished it, 109-97. "We played probably our best playoff game," Daly told the writers afterward. "We were aggressive offensively and defensively, particularly on offense."

"It's nice," Thomas agreed, "but we know from experience that it takes four. We have one and there are six games left."

Once bitten, twice shy, the Bad Boys weren't about to let their spirits soar just because of an opening home-court win, no matter how much the Lakers offense had struggled against Detroit's D. The big effort had come from Mahorn, who harassed James Worthy into 6-for-18 shooting. "Their shots just didn't fall," Dumars said. "We take no credit in stopping them."

As Daly expected, the Lakers snapped right back in Game Two to pound the boards and take a strong first-quarter lead. But Dumars got hot with 24 points in the first half (he would finish with 33) to keep Detroit close. L.A. held a 62-56 lead at intermission; Michael Cooper, Scott's backup, was hitting; and Magic had that look in his eye. But events turned upside down in the third. With about four minutes left, Salley blocked a Mychal Thompson shot, starting the Detroit fastbreak. Magic dropped

Isiah and Magic continued their pre-game bussing from '88.

64

Michael Cooper subbed for Byron Scott.

back to play defense, and in so doing, pulled his hamstring. He sensed immediately that the injury was serious and flailed at the air in frustration (showing a dramatic flair for which comedian Arsenio Hall would mercilessly tease him later in the summer). Magic didn't return after

"I wanted to play so bad, but I just could not. I could not make the cuts, defensively, that I had to make."

—Magic Johnson

that. "I felt a twinge early in the third quarter but thought everything was okay," Johnson said later of the injury. "Then on that last play I pulled it trying to get back on defense."

The Pistons had made the bucket on the break to tie the game at 75, but the Lakers used the setback for momentum, charging to a 90-81 lead late in the third. But the Bad Boys had owned the fourth through most of the playoffs, and Game Two was no different. The Lakers opened the period with three missed baskets and an offensive foul, as Detroit first tied the game, then went up 102-95.

Next it was the Pistons' turn to miss and mess up, as Thompson led a Los Angeles comeback. The final snafu came with a 24-second violation by Detroit, giving the Lakers the ball with eight seconds left. Down 106-104, they had a chance to tie or maybe even win it. The tie looked good when Worthy was fouled and went to the line.

There, the exhaustion caught up with the MVP of the 1988 Finals. He missed the first and made the second, leaving the Lakers short at 106-105. Thomas hit two free throws with a second remaining for the final, 108-105.

Things looked good for the Homes

Magic's injury dampened hopes for Three-peat.

with a 2-0 lead. Damn good. Only nobody was saying that as the series headed to L.A. The most the writers would get out of anybody was a batch of pasty cliches. Stuff about needing four wins to get the rings. In years past, you might have seen signs of real giddiness from the Pistons. But they had learned their lessons well. Oh, a tinge of glee escaped here and there. The game faces did most of

the work for them. After wearing the mask for a year, they would have to keep them on only three more days if they played things right.

Besides, the immediate speculation centered on Magic. Could he play?

He tried.

But he left the game in the first quarter with the Lakers leading 11-8. "I wanted to play so bad, but I just could not," Johnson said later. "I

The Detroit bench helped do in the Lakers. (Einstein photo)

could not make the cuts, defensively, that I had to make."

"He made a heck of an effort," Dumars said, "but it just wasn't there. You could tell by his motion. One time, the ball was right there a couple feet away, and he just couldn't get it."

Without him, the Lakers still did a fair imitation of a championship contender. Worthy scored 26, and Kareem played out of his 42-year-old

body, scoring 24 points with 13 rebounds. The only veteran in the backcourt, Cooper had 13 assists and 15 points. Grand as it was, that didn't do it.

For starters, there was Dennis Rodman, wracked by painful back spasms, getting 19 rebounds between gasps, going to the sideline for rubdowns, then coming back in for another outburst of superhype,

Worming his way inside the Lakers interior defense for offensive boards.

That, of course, was the behind-the-scenes work. The marquee effort came from the guards. Once again, the Detroit backcourt played like Gremlins. Joe D. hit for 31, including a blind, unconscious, Super Bad third quarter, in which he scored 17 consecutive points (21 in all for the period). The Lakers had trouble

Once again, the Detroit backcourt played like Gremlins. Joe D. hit for 31, including a blind, unconscious, Super Bad third quarter, in which he scored 17 consecutive points (21 in all for the period).

switching on defense and left him open repeatedly. Joe was obliged to do the damage.

And when Joe went to his seat for a blow, Vinnie picked up the whirlwind and waved it about him like a cape, scoring 13 points in the crucial fourth period (he finished with 17).

Isiah pitched in 26 with eight assists. Much of his best work came in the clutch, six key points and three assists. Only problem was, so did his only real mistakes of the afternoon. He threw a bad pass with the Pistons leading 103-102.

Still, things seemed pretty secure with 2:06 left when Vinnie hit one of his big-time jumpers to give Detroit a 109-104 lead. They maintained that 5-point margin until 15 seconds remained, when Thomas allowed A.C. Green to tie him up and steal the ball. Thomas then fouled the Lakers David Rivers, who made both, pulling L.A. to 113-110 with 13 seconds left.

Dumars came back in the game then, and at nine seconds, he tipped the ball out of bounds, giving the Lakers a shot at the tie.

Up to this game, Rivers had played only eight minutes in the playoffs, none of it during serious time. But with the injuries, the rookie suddenly found himself with lots of prime time. It doesn't get any more prime than being the number-one option on a last-second three-pointer. The Pistons certainly didn't expect Rivers to be the option.

"He got away from me," Dumars said of Rivers. "I let up a little because when he broke, I let him go.

Salley and Rodman took the Pistons from good to best.

Rodman made Worthy work.

I thought, 'He can't be the first option, so I am going to take a look and see where the ball is going.' I turned back and the ball was going right to him. Then I knew I had to react. I knew he wouldn't be going to the goal because they needed three. I can't even think of the last time I blocked a shot. It was just instinct. I was a good ways from him. It's amazing what you do in pressure situations."

From about eight feet to Rivers' left, Dumars wheeled about and lunged at the shot. Not only did he block it, he then landed and bounded to his left to save it from going out of bounds. "It just kind of hung in the air forever," he said of his saving the ball.

"That was a first team All-

Defensive play right there," Laimbeer said afterward. "To block the shot, yeah everybody blocks shots, but to block the shot and save the ball to your teammate—that's a big play. That's a play you win championships with."

Not to mention MVP awards. "It would be great," Joe admitted when asked about it. "I don't want to down play it, but... Championship ring. That's what you play for. As a kid you watch on television. I've seen so many people win it. People are so happy when they win it. That's the main thing right now."

The defensive play seemed to seal the award for Dumars, especially when combined with his offensive performance against the Lakers. "I

just happened to get into one of those zones where a couple of shots went down and I wanted to touch the ball everytime it came down the floor," he said of his third-quarter scoring.

"Was it a case where you would talk to Isiah and say, 'I'm hot' ?" a writer asked. "Or does he just know that?"

"He knows it," Dumars said. "At one point he asked me, 'What do you want?', meaning what play do I want. I said, 'Just the ball.' That's about how it was, 'Just give me the ball.' "

Down 3-0, the Lakers still talked of making history. Specifically, they would have to be the first team to ever overcome a three-game deficit. Tony Campbell, who had filled in admirably at guard for Scott, asserted

Kareem found the old range in Game 3.

Vinnie did a lot of the late damage.

> **"It's like you have a real nice sports car and a great driver, and then all of a sudden you have to find somebody who has been driving a bus to be a driver. That's a learning experience."**
>
> **—Kareem Abdul Jabbar**

that such a comeback was in the works.

Wiser voices weren't quite so optimistic.

"It's like you have a real nice sports car and a great driver," Kareem said of the Lakers' circumstances, "and then all of a sudden you have to find somebody who has been driving a bus to be a driver. That's a learning experience."

Going in the Glitz Kids knew things would be tough. Pat Riley told Worthy that he would have to up his game a few notches and get the Lakers a win. Riley reminded Worthy how his efforts had paid off in '88.

Worthy remembered. Dude damn near killed Detroit in Game Four. Scored 40, on 17 of 26 from the floor, and that with Mahorn jawing in his face every other step of the way.

The crowd had come expecting an event, Kareem's final game. The big center conducted his final warmup, his bald pate glistening a regal green and red from the Forum lights. He was composed, spending much of the session standing silently in a half slouch, his hand on his hip. The Cap did one final finger roll and headed down to the bench. With that signal, the team followed, igniting a growing applause that spread across the Forum crowd. The spectators were slick, Movie Time types, California boys and girls, but over the years the Lakers had taught them how to get rowdy.

Back in the Palace of Auburn Hills, a sell-out crowd was getting in a

When Magic tried a comeback, Joe was ready with the "D".

practice session watching the game on the big screen. Over the season, they had learned to loosen their $100 ties. But the playoffs had robbed them of the big blowout, because the sweeps meant the Bad Boys won each round on the road. So they gathered for the big one. The floor was empty, but they worked on their rowdiness anyway.

Once the game started, there was plenty to keep them pumped, even if the pattern was familiar. Mahorn and

Cooper mixed it up in the first period, drawing a double technical. With Worthy playing out of his mind, the Lakers took a 35-23 lead at the end of the first. Detroit missed free throws like they were dentist appointments, 11 in all in the first half. But Vinnie made one to close out the scoring with L.A. leading 55-49 at intermission.

True to The Pattern, the Bad Ones jumped out in the third, starting with an opening trey by Mr. Tippy Toes.

True to The Pattern, the Bad Ones jumped out in the third, starting with an opening trey by Mr. Tippy Toes. Mahorn then scored four quick points, and the Pistons took a 59-58 lead moments later when Dumars hit a driving bank shot, drew the foul and made the throw, giving him 19 points on the evening.

Mahorn then scored four quick points, and the Pistons took a 59-58 lead moments later when Dumars hit a driving bank shot, drew the foul and made the throw, giving him 19 points

on the evening. Mahorn followed that with another bucket, and suddenly it was time-out L.A.

When Worthy blasted them back into the lead later in the quarter, the crowd got loud with a chant of "Three-peat." Nice Hollywood stuff. But it would never see the light of reality. They nipped and tucked it a ways from there, all true to The Pattern, which had become bankable by this point in the season.

The Lakers held a 78-76 lead at the end of the third, but they knew it. Everybody in the building knew it. The Bad Boys turned the chores over to James Edwards, who slammed and picked his way along, giving Detroit the lead in the process. As their momentum grew, the Lakers appeared drained.

When Detroit got the ball back with 3:23 left and leading 100-94, the crowd rose to a standing ovation, not

to try and pull a miracle out of exhaustion, just a note of thanks. Kareem came back in the game, but neither side could get it right. The next two minutes was an exchange of missed shots and turnovers.

At 1:37, Kareem broke the chill with a spin move and bank shot, his last NBA points, bringing the Lakers to 100-96. The Big Guy went out at 0:47. Then Laimbeer hit a jumper at 0:28, and the Bad Boys figured it was safe to start hugging during the ensuing time-out. Mahorn stood in the midst of this outbreak, a towel draped over his shoulders, and slowly rotated, looking up into the crowd. Then he raised his arms in triumph, and the TV cameras encircled him.

Through the madness, Daly tried to take charge. Laimbeer was shouting it-ain't-over-'til-it's-over kinds of things. Dumars just sat quietly, his face pressed into a towel.

The Bad Boys answered every challenge.

Riley sent Kareem back in after the timeout. Cooper missed a trey, and Isiah got fouled. With Zeke at the line, Riley sent Orlando Woolridge in for the Cap. It was hug time for the Lakers. Magic came out to meet Kareem. The crowd's applause was both large and warm, and the Pistons all stepped onto the floor, faced the Lakers bench and helped out.

Then Aguirre suddenly grabbed Isiah and began squeezing his head. Looked like he might just pop the sucker right there. Somehow Zeke escaped. Then he turned and hugged Daly. Zeke cried openly for the cameras. Daly later said he forced a tear or two, but it looked like a little more than that. Isiah dropped to his seat and buried his face in a towel, as the TV cameras jumped in over his shoulder.

"Free throws. Let's go," Daly said, breaking the spell.

Isiah went back to the line. Nobody even remembers if he made 'em or not. Who cares? That's the stuff of stat sheets. "Kareem. Kareem. Kareem," the crowd intoned over and over.

Mahorn grabbed Brendan Malone by the suit, giving his nice-looking threads a rough time. Just before the fans rushed the floor, Riley strode down the sideline to shake Daly's hand. Daddy Rich grabbed the victory and squeezed and pumped.

Which was all the sign Isiah needed. He sent the ball zipping into the Forum rafters. High. High. Curling up near the scoreboard. Referee Earl Strom saw it go, kept his eye on it, and dashed toward it out through the crowd, trying to catch it as it came down. Earl doesn't like to lose a game ball, you know.

But it was gone. The crowd had already closed in, and the Pistons were gone, too, headed out through the throng for the locker room and beyond, to discover the excesses of championship, to push the envelope on pure joy.

Just like the game ball, Isiah belonged to the fans. First there was the interview room and the media. Then he squeezed into the hallway and the packed crowd and found a

Zeke and his dream.

seam back to the locker room.

In the midst of this delight, a writer followed him and asked about the dream. Did it exceed reality? he was asked.

"Greater," he said, beaming again. "Far beyond what I could imagine."

POSTSCRIPT

It would be nice to throw a "30" on this thing and end it right there. Dream and reality merged. For a time, it got better, the ride on this crest of celebration. There was Jack McCloskey soaked in champagne and sweat in the locker room. Bill Davidson finding the payoff to his

long-term gamble. The Bad Boys flying full blown, untouched by whistles and fines and print. The team party at Marina del Rey. The crowds in Detroit. The parade. The speeches. The toasts. All of it blown right out, up and across the Michigan sky. One big breath of frustration blasted out until there's nothing left. But then right at the very cap of it, right in the midst of this Ghostbusters-like purging of three decades of Detroit demons, they learned they would be losing Mahorn to the expansion draft and the new franchise, the Minnesota Timberwolves.

Everyone had known someone

Detroit was ready to celebrate.

The President called for a kinder, gentler Pistons.

would be lost. The media had speculated it would be either Vinnie or Edwards. Mahorn had been so much a part of the Pistons mindset, no one really considered him a candidate. He was the Bad Boy. His Badness had been the very core of the Pistons' intimidation.

McCloskey had tried to work a deal, but the Timberwolves wanted a player, not a deal.

With Mahorn's departure, Zeke declared the Bad Boys laid to rest. How could Detroit be Bad without 'Horn'? he asked.

Deep as his disappointment was,

Mahorn gathered his class and joined the team for their visit with President Bush at the White House.

The Pres laughed with them and spoke of a kinder, gentler Pistons. Which they might be.

In your dreams.

Laimbeer prides himself on his mental toughness.

Whatever It Takes

Laimbeer sucks.
That seems like a simple enough declarative sentence here on the page with that period tucked neatly behind it. Yet it's strange how overwhelming those two words become when they're mysteriously and instantly transmitted into the minds of 17,500 fans at Chicago Stadium. They hammer those two words down from the rafters again and again. A loud, aching hammer. Put your fingers in your ears, and still they hammer.

Laim-beer sucks. Laim-beer sucks. Laim-beer sucks.

What's worse, there's no fun in it. Most basketball razzing has its roots in mirth. In Duke's Cameron Stadium, where the students can be a bit cruel, the underpinning of their chants is sophomoric humor. But here, in the Central Division of the NBA, there is nothing but pure disdain. Cold. We hate the sonofabitch.

Laim-beer sucks. Laim-beer sucks. Laim-beer sucks.

They take their time with the words, hoping somehow the message will shove itself into the concentration of the villian.

Bill Laimbeer is at the free throw line. It is the third quarter in Game Six of the Eastern Conference Finals. The score is tied. And while the hammer pounds everywhere around him, Laimbeer fixes his face on the rim and sinks them both, each one a dagger in the throat of the crowd.

Evan "Big Cat" Williams once said of Laimbeer's golf game, "When he's playing regularly, Bill is almost a tour-caliber putter because of his concentration. He told me it was just like shooting free throws. He just locks himself in."

Are you kidding? How'd you like to see Arnie or Nicklaus trying to put the ball in the hole through a rain of hate? They have trouble enough when everybody in the gallery holds his breath and applauds even the misses politely.

"I'm used to being disliked at a national level because I went to Notre Dame," Laimbeer once explained.

Beg your pardon again, but can you think of a time you ever saw the fans rise to their toes, curl their lips

> **"I play smart. I play hard. If either will get the other guy out of his game, get him mad, hey, that's to my advantage. I don't have too many advantages. I have to do what will get me by. Put it this way: I play to win. Whatever it takes."**
>
> **—Bill Laimbeer**

back over their gums and scream 'til their veins bulged, Notre Dame Sucks. Notre Dame Sucks. Notre Dame Sucks.

In the past, Laimbeer has attempted to shrug off this situation. Like Sacramento's Danny Ainge, another player who inspires crowds to their worst, Laimbeer says he draws motiviation from it, even finds it funny. "It's kind of a joke on our team," he says. "It's like I'm the designated villain everywhere we go. Out-of-town fans are always booing me. Other players don't like me because I play good, hard physical basketball. That's the way I have to play and a lot of players don't like that. They like to go

out, run their plays, shoot and have some fun. They don't want to bang around."

In essence, opponents and their fans perceive the 6'11", 255-pound Laimbeer as a dirty player, a charge that Laimbeer takes in stride. "I play smart," he says. "I play hard. If either will get the other guy out of his game, get him mad, hey, that's to my advantage. I don't have too many advantages. I have to do what will get me by. Put it this way: I play to win. Whatever it takes."

Charlotte Hornets Coach Dick Harter, a former assistant with the Pistons, has long admired Laimbeer for just those reasons, which are the same reasons opponents despise the Pistons center. "He plays hard all the time," Harter says. "He comes at you. He doesn't give an inch."

"Nobody is more competitive than Bill Laimbeer during the season," Chuck Daly says. "It's what sets him apart."

All of that sounds good, but it's not the sole reason for Laimbeer's special relationship with out-of-town crowds.

In April, Bob Ryan, the dean of pro basketball writers in Boston, a city that holds no love for Laimbeer, was doing a pre-game talk show on the Cleveland Cavaliers radio network. Asked about the Detroit "Bad Boys," Ryan offered the opinion that Laimbeer was merely irritating while Rick Mahorn was truly dangerous. The league should do something about Mahorn, Ryan said.

Many fans and media types would agree that when it gets right down to it, Mahorn is far more physical. Yet Mahorn during his tenure as the baddest of the Bad Boys was seldom the target of unadulterated spite.

And just minutes after Ryan's

interview, the Cleveland crowd was pounding Laimbeer, not Mahorn, with that familiar chant.

Beyond the physical play, it's the irritation factor that separates Laimbeer from other competitors. It's his twinkle-toed perimeter shot, and his complaining to officials. And like Ainge, Laimbeer is a man of expressions and grimaces, leading to charges that he's a whiner.

With all of these things combining to create his on-court persona, Bill Laimbeer has been drawing the wrath of crowds for a few seasons now. In fact, this might be an old story, except that the intensity of disdain seems to grow each year, and it reached new limits in last spring's playoffs.

For the 1989-90 season, Pistons General Manager Jack McCloskey is hoping to defuse some of the issue as the team moves away from its Bad Boy image and marketing tag. Yet Laimbeer's situation existed well before anyone thought of the Bad Boy bit, and it likely will exist long afterward, probably into his retirement years.

Matt Dobek, the Pistons director of public relations who has watched Laimbeer's standoff with the crowds for several years, has come to a conclusion. It's pretty simple: Bill Laimbeer is the most hated athlete in America.

Danny Ainge is disliked, Dobek points out, but the Boston Celtics traded Ainge to Sacramento last season. And maybe John McEnroe was more despised in his heyday. But McEnroe's time of seething villainy has passed.

The mantle, it seems, has fallen to Bill Laimbeer.

While he may be saying he doesn't mind the verbal abuse, his growing frustration was apparent last spring. Laimbeer seemed to face searing controversy with each round of the playoffs.

The Pistons opened with Boston, and every Pistons fan knows the special feelings Laimbeer and Celtics center Robert Parish hold for each other. Parish's standing comment for years has been: "I was always taught that if you can't say something nice about someone, then don't say anything at all. So I'm saying nothing at all."

The two battled in the 1987 playoffs and did so again to open the

Beantown has special feelings for Bill. (Lipofsky photo)

The playoffs brought plenty of controversy for Laimbeer.

1988-89 season, resulting in both being ejected from a game in Boston Garden.

Yet, the Celtics playoff series, which ended in a three-game sweep, was mild compared to what followed. In fact, fans in Boston Garden seemed almost civil to Laimbeer. At least their boos didn't do permanent damage to the tympanum.

At Milwaukee, however, things turned mean during game three of the second round, when Bucks forward Larry Krystkowiak suffered a severe knee injury while breaking to the basket near Laimbeer. At the time, the crowd and Bucks Coach Del Harris exploded with anger. Although videotaped replays of the incident confirmed there was little or no contact between Laimbeer and Krystkowiak, Harris blasted Laimbeer after the game. The hatred didn't dissipate in game four, when the crowd's cheer of choice was, you guessed it, "Laim-beer sucks."

Against Chicago in the East finals, trouble struck again. This time it came in game six. Laimbeer set himself to rebound, and Bulls forward Scottie Pippen crashed the boards from behind, catching Laimbeer's elbow in the right eye in the process.

Pippen crumpled to the floor, and although he suffered no permanent damage, he didn't return to the game, going instead to the hospital where he stayed overnight for observation of his concussion.

Again, replays showed conclusively that the contact was inadvertent, but the crowd would have none of it. In their mass opinion, Laimbeer, well, you know.

And afterward in the Chicago locker room, Bulls Coach Doug Collins railed against what he called Laimbeer's dirty play. Reporters immediately brought Collins' colorful comments to Laimbeer, who was nonplussed. He replied that he didn't even know Pippen had been injured until he ran to the other end of the court and looked back to see the trainers gathered around him.

By the finals, the battering of the season seemed to have taken its toll. Laimbeer's play was suffering, and he

Laimbeer finds a friendly crowd in the Palace.

had become increasingly testy with reporters.

After the Pistons swept the series against the Lakers, he brought his frustrations to the post-game interview with the national media. "Vindication, that's the word I've been using all along," he told the gathering. "Everybody on this team has taken a lot of abuse, from you and from the fans. We get a lot of heat, you call us thugs and a lot of names you can't print, though you printed them anyway. So it is vindication to finally win the championship. We play a physical style of basketball, and you can call us what you want but we are the champions. That's all that matters."

Tough as it may be some nights, Bill is determined to be Bill, just as he's determined not to be affected by the noise.

"We're in the entertainment business, and the fans have a right to boo the visiting team," he said last season. "They like to pick out one guy in particular, and I just happen to be that guy.

"I guess it's because I'm a fierce competitor. But I'm not going to change any."

Certainly he isn't going to change now that the Pistons are world champions. Not after the long, tough road Laimbeer has taken to get to the top. The championship was the qualifying factor of his mission.

Some opponents object to Bill's style.

"All my career, people told me the rule of thumb is that you must have a dominating center to win it all," he told the media during the press conference after the championship. "It was a myth. I never believed that. Teams win NBA championships, and competitors win NBA championships. We proved that here."

At the heart of what drives Bill Laimbeer is the pride he takes in his game. That may sound strange to some, because his game is, well, strange.

He's a center, a strong defensive-rebounder, with the offensive skills of a guard. Probably his best shot is that tippy-toes three pointer, but late last year he surprised people by showing a new, athletic approach to the game, mostly when teams tried to defend him with guards and small forwards.

The real pride Laimbeer takes in his game is his rebounding and consistency, which is another reason the past season brought him a personal disappointment. After his January fight with Cleveland center Brad Daugherty, the league suspended both players for one game, which brought to an end Laimbeer's streak of playing 685 straight games, the fourth longest in league history.

He had needed only 22 more consecutive games to pass former NBA great Dolph Schayes (706). Randy Smith is tops with 906 and John Kerr is second at 844.

"The thing I like most about streak," he said, "is that I think players and fans will remember me for being a durable guy in this league, for being able to play every night, for playing over the pain."

That, of course, is what has made Laimbeer immensely valuable to the Pistons. Other centers are flashy and dominant. Just about all of them get a better reception on the road.

But Laimbeer is there night in, night out, doing the dirty work. "That's the tough thing about this game," he said. "It's such a tough mental grind. You have to be on your toes every minute of every game or you can be embarrassed. And I don't like to be embarrassed."

Avoiding that red face seems to

Laimbeer's offense is geared for the perimeter.

His rebounding has been a Pistons' staple.

have been sufficient motivation for him. Since coming to Detroit in a 1982 trade with Cleveland, Laimbeer has put in better than 2,800 minutes per season, averaging better than 16 points and 11 rebounds.

Nobody ever thought he would be that good.

"Laimbeer flops around like a fish out there," Cedric Maxwell once said. That was pretty much the attitude that had followed big Bill around most of his career.

Born in Boston, he was raised a child of wealth in California. "I'm the only player in the NBA who makes less money than his father," he once said. Actually Bill Laimbeer Sr., an executive vice president of Owens-Illinois, today earns about half of his son's $600,000 annual salary.

Still, Laimbeer's experiences were far different from the average NBA player. "When I first met him he acted exactly like a rich kid from the suburbs," Isiah Thomas said two seasons ago. "He knew how to eat lobster and go to the beach. But now he doesn't think quite so white anymore."

Laimbeer agreed. "Isiah's a great guy," he said. "We educate one another. We'll be shooting baskets and he'll say, 'Man, where I grew up the rims were bent and we didn't have any nets.' And I'll say, 'Really? I just went into my private court in the backyard."

Despite what some see as the handicap of affluence, Laimbeer starred in both football and basketball in high school in Palos Verdes. "I guess it was an easy life for Bill," his father said. "But he found his own niche and succeeded in it. Most lily-white kids, you know, don't know how to mix it up."

He was big enough and good enough to get a variety of scholarship offers, from which he picked Notre

Avoiding that red face seems to have been sufficient motivation for him. Since coming to Detroit in a 1982 trade with Cleveland, Laimbeer has put in better than 2,800 minutes per season, averaging better than 16 points and 11 rebounds.
Nobody ever thought he would be that good.

Dame. As a freshman in 1975-76, he averaged 8.5 points in 10 games for the Irish. But he ran into academic trouble and transferred to Owens Tech, where he worked on his grades.

Family is Laimbeer's retreat.

He and Mahorn led the Bad Boys sweep.

He returned to Notre Dame, and for the next two years he was a meat-and-potatoes kind of guy for the Irish, averaging about seven points a game. He explains this performance by saying he was never allowed to show his abilities in college.

His size got him noticed by the NBA scouts, and Cleveland made him the 65th players selected in the 1979 draft. He couldn't quite cut it in camp, however, and was advised to play in Italy.

He spent the next season playing for Brescia, averaging 21 points a game while shooting 55 percent from the floor.

He returned to Cleveland the next season, ready to perform. But he averaged only nine points per game for the Cavs. Today, Laimbeer sees the 1982 trade as the move that

opened his basketball life. "Getting to Detroit and playing with guys like Isiah certainly helped my game," he said. "I don't know if I would have improved as much in Cleveland."

For 1982-83, he gave Detroit 13.6 points per game and 12.5 rebounds. If you know anything about Pistons basketball in those days, you know Laimbeer had found a home.

His trademark became his rebounding. He moved immediately into the upper echelon of rebounders in the NBA, and in 1986, he led the league. "What I do, I do well," he said at the time. "I rebound. That's my pride. It's not how, it's how many."

Observers continue to marvel at this because Laimbeer is not a leaper. Yet he is a master of technique. "Rebounding is hands and balance," former Cleveland coach

George Karl said. "Laimbeer holds his position and jumps only the four inches he has to."

"Bill's the epitome of the guy running in the sand," Chuck Daly once remarked. "Frankly, he's a blue collar worker. Bill knows his limitations. It takes an intelligent player to understand that."

It also takes a tough mind to turn off the crowds. After each season, Laimbeer retreats to his privacy to lick his wounds and spend time with his wife and two children. He plays golf, does a little fishing and refuses to give a minute of this precious freedom to basketball. It's not hard to understand why. Maybe when he's lost in the quiet of a lake or the earthy stillness of golf course, Laimbeer can finally get the ringing hammer of that chant out of his ears.

Top right—The
Microwave plays
great defense, too.
Top left—Buddha
and Worm battle for
the rebound.
Right—Salley kicks
the ball out.

Name That Bench

Just when you think that great sports nicknames are a thing of the past along come the Detroit Pistons with a bench that sounds like a high-tech nightmare.

Worm. Spider. Microwave. Buddha.

Buddha?

Make that a high-tech nightmare while dozing in an Eastern temple.

It wasn't too long ago that the pundits thought monikers were for baseball old-timers and football legends. You know. The Babe. Joltin' Joe. Slingin' Sammy. Alan "The Horse" Ameche. Guys like that.

Sure, there was an occasional modern breakthrough, such as "Goose" Gossage or "The Bird" Fidrych, but that was baseball.

Pro basketball offered few nicknames. Maybe Magic and Spud and Chief. But outside of that, the game had only a boring collection of Larrys and Michaels and Bills and Bobs.

Then, in two short seasons, the Bad Boys changed all that. They put forth so many nicknames the press took to callin 'em the Garbage Pail Kids.

Which is fine, except that sounds kind of cuddly and cute, or at least chummy. If you saw the Bad Boys last season, they were anything but chummy. Maybe Cossacks in short pants, or Hell's Angels in high-top sneakers. But never chummy.

Anyway, a nickname is only as good as who's wearing it. In the case of Detroit's bench, it isn't really a matter of good. Awesome would be a more appropriate word. When Chuck Daly went to his subs during Pistons games last season, it seemed he was kicking the team into overdrive. Detroit's play zoomed off to a new level, leaving opponents looking weak-kneed and bewildered.

Whether it was the Boston Celtics or the Miami Heat, the effect was the same. The Motor City blast-off left everybody in the dust.

Come to think of it, that's just what you'd expect of a high-tech nightmare.

"My friends knew I was real hyper. Real hyper. They knew I wouldn't settle down, I wouldn't sleep. I'd just keep going."

"And now I just focus my energy in something I love to do. Now, I just play basketball, go out there and have a lot of fun and enjoy."

—Dennis Rodman

WORM

Nobody in Detroit is more responsible for this mayhem than Dennis Rodman, a.k.a. "The Worm", so named in his youth for his twisting and turning and gyrating at a pinball machine.

He brings that same antsiness to his roundball game, which features an unhealthy fascination with rebounding, a defensive style that borders on a personality disorder, and more thunder dunks than a mid summer storm.

Feeding this behavior is a natural hyperactivity, which makes you wonder how he ever survived before he found basketball. "My friends knew I was real hyper. Real hyper," he says of his days as a teenager in Dallas, Texas. "They knew I wouldn't settle down, I wouldn't sleep. I'd just keep going.

"And now I just focus my energy in something I love to do. Now, I just play basketball, go out there and have a lot of fun and enjoy."

That joy is obvious in his gait, which seems almost out of character with the Worm. In warmups, he runs erect, proudly, springing off each toe, then kicking his heels up behind him daintily. There is almost something Victorian in his posture as he jogs, something old-fashioned, something prim, smacking of *Casey At The Bat* and barbershop quartets, or some other cockiness from a lost era. The Worm is a throwback...

Until you see him fill the lane on the fastbreak, when he blows off all the old-fashioned pretensions. Then he's just a blur. Imagine yourself as Zeke in the center running the break, Rodman to your right. You encounter a defender at the key and toss a fat one up there, and Worm curls from the right, rising high. Damn, it seems he's above the glass, taking the ball and putting it down with a tomahawk. He lands with a jet skid, a tight angle, falls back a bit, catches himself with his left hand, and as he rights himself, shoots the right hand skyward, jutting his index finger. He's number one. Or somebody is number one. Anyway, before you can blink, the hyperactivity has refilled his tanks, and he circles and zooms back upcourt, where he can have some real fun and play defense, making somebody's night miserable.

Dennis Rodman is the past and the future all in one.

There is not a pure basketball fan in America, not even one with the greenest of Celtic hearts, who doesn't

The name is Rodman, as in Rebound.

love the way Rodman plays. He was said to have spent a good part of his early 20s, before he was discovered, pounding fenders in a Dallas body shop. You can see some of that in his game.

Like any smart player with unrefined offensive skills, he makes his living on the boards, particularly the offensive boards. Unlike many inside players, he's not into pettiness. No sly little tricks. He's not much of a grabber. Rather than making contact, he's into avoiding it. When the Pistons have the ball, he often backs away from the lane, his hands on his hips, his eyes always on the guards working the ball on the perimeter. He watches the ball intently, waiting to make his move, to get that special little piece of position for an offensive rebound. This is his primary study, his soul's joy of joys.

Chick Hearn, the Lakers veteran radio man, watched the 6'8" Rodman during the NBA Finals last spring and declared him the best rebounder in the game.

"The best rebounder?" Rodman asked when told of the comment. "In the game? You mean they put me in front of Oakley, Barkley, all those guys? I wouldn't say that. I think I'm one of the best ones, one of the the top ten. But, I can't be the best rebounder. I'm just in a situation where they need my rebounding here. I rebound with the best of them even though I am not as bulky as some guys. I use my ability to jump and use my quickness to get around guys."

That quickness, says Chuck Daly, is one of the things that sets Rodman apart from the other players in the league. It also helps that pro basketball seems to have lost the art of boxing out. But then again, can you imagine trying to put a body on the Worm?

The reason few people box out is that rebounding has come to be considered a thankless task. But that's no problem for the Worm. Sometimes, when he sneaks in and steals an offensive rebound, he'll

dribble out to the perimeter, stand there with the ball in one palm and punch the air with his other fist. He usually does this in the Palace, where the crowd bathes him in warm applause, and he can soak in the ineffable glow of limelight.

His defense is far too workmanlike to allow for such recompense. Like the greatest, he plays it foremost with his feet but keeps his hands and arms moving, eager to snatch the ball. And every time his opponent beats him, Dennis Rodman takes it as a personal affront to his humanity, or his Wormliness.

It was after the 1987 season, after he made his regrettable comment that Larry Bird was overrated, that Rodman decided to make defense his calling card. Not because Chuck Daly suggested it. "I just came to training camp and said, 'Hey, I want to play defense,' " Rodman says. "Then the [1988] playoffs really got me going. I just told myself, 'It's time to start focusing on something you really want to do.' I just feel like defense is what I really want to do."

His defensive ability is all the more remarkable when you consider that he played no high school basketball. He didn't find the organized game until an assitant coach spotted him and recruited him for Cooke County Junior College in Gainesville, Texas. He averaged 17.6 points in one season there, then moved on to Southeastern Oklahoma, where he put up great numbers, better than 25 points and 15 rebounds per game for three seasons. He led the NAIA in scoring for 1985 and '86, which was enough to get him noticed by the Pistons, who made him the 27th player (second round) selected in the 1986 draft.

Since then, Rodman has developed into a marvelously versatile sub. Quick enough to stay with Michael Jordan or any other big guard/small forward in the league, motivated enough to play power forward. Even tough enough to jump a little center.

His defensive game has become a wonder of quick assembly. He describes his approach as "focusing in on the guys that I have to play and bearing down on what I need to do to stop this guy. Just having the hunger and the desire to want to do the job. Because not many guys in the league want to play defense. Not many guys want to do that. If you can kind of put it in your mind and say, 'Hey I got to play defense because I know I'm not going to score as much, I know I'm not going to the ball on offense.' So why would I exert myself too much on offense when I can exert myself on defense?"

Chuck Daly couldn't be more pleased if he had asked the question himself.

Which brings us down to the essence of Rodman. The most hyper facet of this very hyper guy is his motivation.

It was strong enough to keep him going in last year's Finals when he was wracked by back spasms that would have sidelined just about any other NBA player.

But come to think of it, no other NBA player had spent his young adulthood pounding those fenders in that Dallas body shop.

THE MICROWAVE

Yes, yes, you've heard of the Microwave, that ball of muscle who heats up the Pistons offense in a hurry. But what about his alter ego to the second power, THE DEEP FREEZE.

Yes, ladies and gents, most people don't realize it, but Vinnie Johnson is one heck of a defensive player, too. He gets the pub for that automatic shot, but during last year's Eastern Conference finals, Vinnie was closer to Michael Jordan than a brother.

"All people talk about is his offense," Isiah Thomas says of the Microwave. "But he is a great defensive player, too."

Defense has always been a big part of his game, Vinnie says. "It just hasn't been recognized as much because I was so effective offensively. That's because people tend to remember some of the shots I make or some of the rolls I get on. But, I've always been a pretty decent

defensive player. I'm not that tall, but I'm pretty quick for my size. A lot of people don't realize that, and I have a good strong body. I can use my body as far as not letting guys get the position they like to get. I've got good leaping ability, so I make it tough on guys to shoot over me. It is not as easy as it seems sometimes."

He fashioned his incredible offensive game on the playgrounds of Brooklyn as a teenager. He got his defensive skills there, too. The game was one-on-one. The stakes were high for a city kid: Personal pride and self-worth. "Growing up in New York is first defense," Vinnie says, "because if somebody shake you and bake you and then take you and then you have a group of people around cheering, that's embarrassing. You don't want to get embarrassed, so you learn how to play defense quick growing up in New York."

You don't want to get embarrassed

as a Detroit Piston because good defensive skills mean playing time. Night in, night out, Vinnie's defense gets a good workout. Opposing coaches seem to believe the best way to wear down a hot offensive player is to make him work on defense.

"That's a strategy of a lot of coaches," Vinnie says.

But let's be frank, 31-year-old Vinnie Johnson isn't in the game because he's a defensive stopper. He has survived and thrived in pro basketball because of his offensive abilities. In the Pistons' drive to the World Championship last year, Daly often called on the Microwave to heat the team's offense with his searing scoring abilities.

"The players around the league fear him," Thomas says. "It seems like every time we play the Celtics, Vinnie gets on fire. He gives them that double pump. DJ will have his

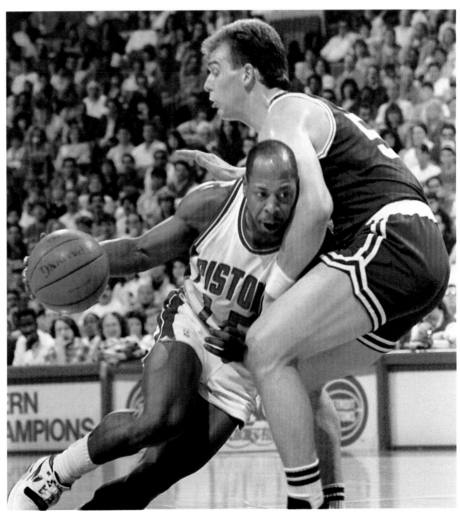

Vinnie is a ball of muscle.

89

hand on the ball, and Vinnie will take it out of his hand and bury it. From like 20 feet."

It was the Celtics, of course, who tagged Vinnie as the Microwave in the first place. Then Boston guard Danny Ainge was impressed with V.J.'s performance in the playoffs a few years back. "If that guy in Chicago is called Refrigerator, then Vinnie is Microwave," Ainge said. "He really heated it up in a hurry."

The Microwave trademark is streak scoring off the bench, big numbers quickly. Usually with people hanging all over him. That, too, is pure Brooklyn. "There was no such thing as an uncontested layup," he said. "You'd get tossed to the cement. You had to learn how to take the shot and get fouled because you'd never get away with calling fouls all the time on the playground. They'd never let you. You just had to learn how to take your hits."

The Pistons came to rely on him more and more down the stretch run to the championship. With injuries to Thomas and Dumars, the Microwave

kept the offense toasty. Even with everyone healthy, he remained just as important, giving Detroit incredible scoring off the bench, not to mention the mental lift his performances brought to his teammates. "I know he gets my juices running," Isiah Thomas said. "Vinnie is fun when he gets going. We just tell him to take every shot. We all screen for him and he just goes crazy."

"If I hit two or three in a row, I am going to look for that shot," Vinnie says. "And I don't care how big or strong he is, I'm gonna take my shot. I am used to taking off-balanced shots, shots that would look difficult to other guys, but if I'm shooting it, I'm shooting it."

Arguably, there is no more entertaining facet of pro basketball today than watching Vinnie fall into his scoring trance. "I sit back and become a fan just like the rest," Joe Dumars says. "He's unreal. He gets unconscious. You start wondering what he could possibly do next."

Chuck Daly agrees, but coach that he is, he finds reason for concern in

this. "It's fascinating for everybody in the whole building," Daly said. "He's unstoppable. But it can act as a double-edged sword for us, too. Everybody stands around and admires Vinnie. It's tough not to respond that way. It sort of takes everybody out of the offense. But when he's hot, you've still got to ride him."

Johnson becomes more singular with each passing season. What other player has averaged double figures over his career while playing almost exclusively as a sub? In that regard, he stands alone. It isn't an easy accomplishment. Having the confidence of a scorer and the patience of a sub makes for an uneasy combination. Learning to deal with life on the bench has been vital to his development. "It was a little difficult at first," he said. "Growing up and coming out of high school and college I was always used to being the man. It was an adjustment in the first two or three years, but once I accepted the role, things came easy to me."

In most places, bench players are held in lower esteem than the starters. The sixth man has been valued around the league for years, but the Pistons have expanded the concept to nine and 10 quality players. Vinnie's skills have been a major part of that development, for which the championship was the ultimate prize. That still doesn't mean that in his heart of hearts, Vinnie has abandoned dreams of being a starter.

"Sometimes," he says, "I think about not getting some of the credit or respect that I think I deserve, but that's just part of the business. I am just put into this position. That is just the way it's going to be. And when you expect that and know that's the way it's going to be, you're going to have some good games and you're going to be consistent, and you're not going to be tripping over yourself about why things are a certain way."

That attitude pervades the entire Detroit bench. From Rodman to Vinnie to Buddha to Spider. They've found an identity within an identity. More often than not, these subs

Vinnie plays a lot of prime time.

played the key late minutes for Detroit in playoff games. And now, where most coaches worry about breaking up a starting five, Chuck Daly has to think about holding together a finishing four.

SPIDER

The other factor in this finishing four is the Spider. He doesn't have eight legs, but when he shifts into his whirling pivot, John Salley sometimes seems like he has four arms and four legs. He has an unusually wide stance, a wide base, for a skinny seven-footer. It's the very foundation of his wonderful shot-blocking agility.

About the only thing more wonderful than this agility is Salley's gift of gab. The humor rolls off his conversation in snappy little quips. If the NBA were his high school, Salley would claim a lot of the superlatives. Wittiest. Friendliest. Most-charming.

Yet he probably wouldn't be in the running for Most Likely to Succeed. At least not yet anyway. It has been thought for some time that his good nature has gotten in the way of his good game.

Marty Blake, the NBA's director of scouting had this assessment as Spider entered the league: "Salley has good speed, and he can block shots, and he's a good jumper. People say that his attention span is short—well, I look at him physically and he's got great potential. He's not the answer, but he's going to help a team a little, and that's all you need."

Amazing prophet, that fellow Blake.

Chuck Daly also had an analysis after Salley's first six games in the league: "He lacks strength. He needs to develop a shot. He's an outstanding passer, but that's based on the fact that he doesn't want to shoot. And in this league you can't do one if you don't do the other."

Daly added another observation: "He'll find his way."

They've all been right about John Salley, it seems. The last remark is perhaps the most prophetic. Salley has found his way. The path hasn't been direct by any means. In fact, he

Salley has learned to be aggressive.

appeared quite lost at times. But heading into the 1989-90 season, he seems closer than ever to getting there.

Salley, who earned an Industrial Management degree at Georgia Tech, came to the Pistons as the eleventh pick of the 1986 draft. His immediate impact was negligible, but Chuck Daly showed patience and gave him playing time. Like many rookies, Salley's response was inconsistency.

This inconsistency, however, carried well into his second season, 1987-88, and his effort might have been written off altogether if it hadn't been for his strong showing in the '88 playoffs. He played a solid role in the Pistons trip to the NBA Finals.

As a result, expectations were again high for 1988-89, his third season, but again the inconsistencies flared. He spent much of the winter playing under the cloud of trade rumors. Then, in the spring, Salley saw more playing time and even started a run of several games. But just when he began to show some consistency, a broken left ankle sidelined him for a month. The ankle had troubled Salley throughout

February. Then as the team entered March, medical tests revealed the fracture. As a result, Salley watched the team's incredible March turnaround from the bench.

He returned in April and found himself near the bottom of Daly's priorities. He played a smattering of garbage seconds as Detroit claimed the Central Division title in Cleveland in mid-April, but by the playoffs, he had found his stride again.

In the first game against the Celtics, he had 15 points, seven rebounds and six blocked shots. "He was sensational," Daly said afterward, but the coach's tone remained unconvinced.

The next day at practice, the coach discussed Salley again. "When he started for us he did an outstanding job the whole time," Daly said. "He just is not built to be a starter, physically. And then he got hurt, lost 15 games, when he fractured a foot, after having started 15 games or so. And I think it has to do with the way he's built. He's not physically a strong person."

The consistency remained a factor, as had Salley's seeming inability to improve, Daly said. "He has stayed about the same. I was hoping for a little more improvement in some areas [over the season], but I didn't really see any improvement in any particular area. He's a peculiar player. When he's playing well like that, he can be as good as there is. But it comes and goes. It's very elusive, at least for me."

"When you don't see improvement in a guy at this point in his career, do you worry about what his future may hold?" a Boston writer asked the coach.

"No," Daly said, "because he's good enough to play or start in the NBA. It's like dieting, it's like quitting smoking; he has to make the decision about weights and about improving his low-post game in the off season. It's not going to happen in season. But he's got a great attitude. He's got terrific mental health, probably as good as anyone in the league. He's a great kid. But he's got to decide how hard he wants to work at the game and how much he wants improve. That's his decision. We can't force that on him. It's hard."

Asked about his off-season plans, Salley said, "I have nutritionist working with my diet this summer, and I'll be working out on weights with this trainer. I'm playing basketball this summer. I'm not going to hang out. I'm going to take a week off after we finish playing, and then I'm just going to go back. I think this summer is the most important summer in my career, period."

The next breath, however, brought a round of one-liners. Asked about his inside game, Salley said, "I'm not really into that power stuff. I'd rather just run by you 90 miles-per-hour and dunk it, and run back by you. Roll around you. All that banging stuff, I'd have to take all these steroids to do that."

Ultimately, he kept his sense of humor and still played consistently throughout the playoffs. Daly began to rely on him for shotblocking and interior defense. Salley added his scoring and rebounding as extras. In every series, he was a factor.

With the conclusion of the championship series against the

Lakers, Salley had played 17 games without significant lapses. He had become an important facet of a multifaceted team. The celebration in the locker room in Los Angeles left him struggling for words, perhaps for the first time in his life.

"This shows we're not just a team of All Stars," he said finally. "It's a 12-man team. Chuck treats us all as equals, treats us like human beings. He doesn't take away anybody's confidence. He encourages everybody to do the best and do what they are most competent at doing.

"I had no control over the trade rumors or how I was being treated. So I thought about it and said, 'Hey, when it comes to the time, all I got to do is work my heart out, do what I'm capable of doing, and I'll be okay.' I made a determination to do what I was good at. I wanted to put it on the

court. If I played only 20-25 minutes a game, I wanted to play hard every minute.

"I'm a shot blocker. I've been a shot blocker all my life, and I wanted to make myself available for that. My whole life, I've had agility. And I've had pretty good jumping ability and pretty good timing."

Salley had resisted the team's overtures that he needed to bulk up to play in the NBA, but the season had helped convince him that weightlifting would be important to his future.

"I'm gonna bulk up just for the life of it," he said as the celebration was beginning to subside. "That keeps you stronger throughout the years and helps prevent injuries. I can add the weight and keep my athleticism. I think my game is going to get better and better over the years."

Vintage Spider.

It wasn't one of his trademark quips, but the words were just the kind to make Chuck Daly smile.

BUDDHA

His Fu Manchu has brought him the name Buddha, but that's about James Edwards' only connection to The Enlightened One. The original Buddha was apparently short and somewhat portly, the kind of guy perfectly suited for contemplating his navel. Edwards, of course, is 263 pounds, but that's spread over his 7'1" frame. Rather than contemplating navels, he's a sophisticate. Any contemplation time he has goes to boating.

But, what the heck, the Fu Manchu is enough for the Bad Boys, so who's gonna argue?

The same can be said for Edwards' game itself. It's hard to find his exact contribution in the statistics. During the '89 playoffs, he averaged about seven points and two rebounds per game. But it was just the seven points and two rebounds that the Pistons happened to need at the time. So what the heck?

Edwards had bounced around quite a bit over his 12-year career before finding a home in Detroit. He came to Motown from Phoenix in a February 1988 trade for Ron Moore and Detroit's second-round pick in 1991.

"It just gives us tremendous insurance," Pistons General Manager Jack McCloskey said at the time. "He can back up Billy [Laimbeer] and if anybody goes down with an injury we've got a veteran center who can also play power forward."

Chuck Daly put it this way: "He gives us another button to push."

That button became the right one in the '88 playoffs. Edwards' presence was a large factor in the Pistons beating the Celtics in Boston Garden in game one of the 1988 Eastern Conference Finals. If nothing else, his role in ending Boston's domination of Detroit made his acquisition worthwhile.

Edwards struggled a bit in the 1988-89 regular season. He sprained

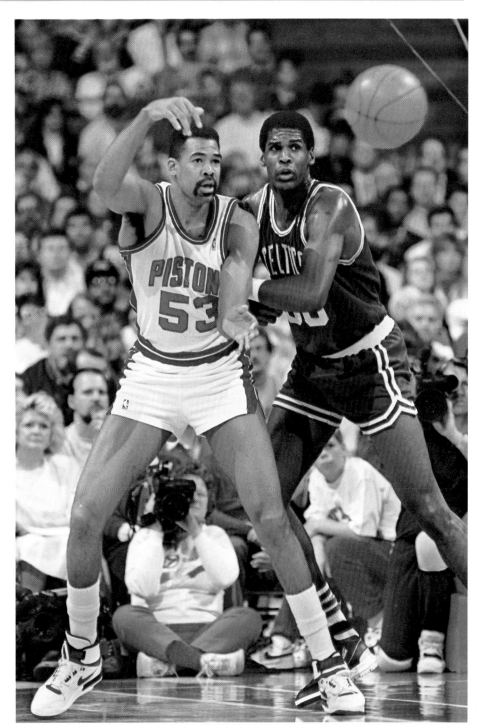

Buddha helped baffle Boston.

his ankle in a November game at Charlotte and never caught up with the rest of the team. His conditioning seemed to keep him a step off the pace throughout much of the season. For the first time in his career, he didn't average in double figures scoring.

Then, once again, he managed to play a larger role in the playoffs. For this upcoming season, Edwards seems a sure bet for more minutes,

with Rick Mahorn having been lost to Minnesota.

Even if he doesn't shine during the regular season, you get the impression the Pistons will be patient enough to keep him around for the playoffs. After all, he's the guy who helped beat Boston.

Plus, they need a name like Buddha to hold down the high tech nightmare.

Trader Jack.

A Talk With Trader Jack

They call him Trader Jack because he's been a bit of a maverick in acquiring players to build the Pistons. And that's true. General Manager Jack McCloskey hasn't been afraid to take bold steps in the front office. Nothing seemed riskier than trading Adrian Dantley for Mark Aguirre last February. Yet McCloskey is hardly a typical sports executive.

Billy Packer, the college basketball analyst for CBS Sports, has known McCloskey since the two coached together at Wake Forest in the mid 1960s. Asked to describe McCloskey, Packer said that Trader Jack was first and foremost a tough old basketball coach, as hard-nosed a competitor as Packer has seen anywhere in the business.

The other impressive thing about McCloskey is his honesty. He's not the kind of guy to fret over the words he chooses. He discusses things as he sees them. He answered the following questions in a series of interviews, which ended in late August.

Q: Are you still celebrating the Pistons' World Championship?

McCloskey: No, not really. I honestly haven't had a chance to thoroughly enjoy the feeling of complete victory. The reason for that is the timing of the expansion draft. That has really put a dampening effect on me.

Q: The Pistons lost Rick Mahorn to the Minnesota Timberwolves in the expansion draft. Unfortunately, you had to inform Mahorn of that development just as the team was celebrating its championship in Detroit. Have you had occasion to speak to Mahorn since?

McCloskey: I talked to him right after the thing. We were in Washington visiting the White House. It's tough. I think he handled it very, very well. He understands the coaches and I had to make a decision. In effect, we were being penalized for having an abundance of good players.

Q: Do you second guess yourself?

McCloskey: Of course not. Still, that doesn't stop it from hurting. I lost a guy who was a great contributor. Just as I would if we had decided on Vinnie Johnson or James Edwards or any other great contributor. We lost a good member of the team.

Q: Do you like Detroit's chances to repeat?

McCloskey: I think we'll be going into camp with the possibility of the best team we've ever had.

Q: Do you expect fallout from the loss of Mahorn.

McCloskey: Everybody said Joe Dumars would be devastated by Adrian Dantley being traded. Joe Dumars was the MVP during the playoffs, probably our MVP throughout the year. Saying there will be fallout is like setting up excuses. Hell, these players are professionals. They're competitors. They want to win.

Q: You've been described as a gambler, a maverick as far as assembling this team. Does that name fit you?

McCloskey: I don't know about a gambler. If you gamble, your odds are always against you. We could have gambled on a lot of trades, and gamble would have been the word.

But we would have been making mistakes.

Q: Many people considered the Dantley deal a gamble.

McCloskey: There was an undercurrent on our team last winter which was not good. We hadn't beaten New York, we were unsuccessful against Cleveland and we hadn't beaten Milwaukee. If we wanted to get out of the East, we were not going to do it with the team we had or with the attitude or mentality that we had. It seemed like we were a divided team, we were not together.

Q: What was your primary concern in making the trade?

McCloskey: Winning. I was convinced we had to make some adjustment somewhere along the line, or we could just not get out of the East. We just weren't going to do it.

Q: Were you worried about Aguirre's image as a spoiled player?

McCloskey: Sure, I was concerned. If we did not have the strong leadership we had on this team I would not have made that trade.

Q: He had to do some bench sitting, yet didn't seem to mind. Did you or Chuck Daly ever talk to Aguirre about that?

McCloskey: No. I did talk to some of our guys, and I said, "I expect you to handle any adverse situation that comes up, and if you can't handle it, then I will." But, I didn't anticipate anything coming up. Aguirre ended up scoring less for us than he ever had, but our team scored more.

Q: Frankly, the media seemed amazed that you had gotten Aguirre, a superstar, to work as a role player.

McCloskey: I don't think Mark Aguirre quite fits that superstar image. I think he is a very talented player. I think there are very few superstars in the league.

Q: He has scored big numbers.

McCloskey: In that context he is, but he is a very suspect player defensively.

Q: Have you seen improvement?

McCloskey: I think he has improved. I think he has tried, and I think he has worked at it. I think he has gotten better. He could be a much better defender than he is, and eventually we hope that he will be. He thinks he is working at it, and he is. I am very pleased with his overall attitude. He was in horrible shape when he got here, but has worked at that, too.

Q: There seemed to be a good bit of friction last season between the Pistons and the office of Rod Thorn, the NBA's vice president for operations. Did Thorn fine the Bad Boys excessively?

McCloskey: I think our guys probably overreacted a little bit as far as Rod is concerned on that. Because Rod is an ex-player, he knows the game, he knows the situations that are involved. But he has got to abide by his instincts and also what the commissioner wants.

Q: Do you think the Pistons were treated fairly?

McCloskey: As far as the fines and everything go, yes. You know, they gotta make the fines. I do think there are some officials in the league that probably become so acutely aware of our reputation... I can show you tapes and tapes and tapes where in the relative situation of contact, one foul would be called against Mahorn where it would not be called against someone else. But, that is the price you have to pay. I really admire Rod. He's got a tough job. He cannot be right.

Q: Do you think the Pistons were getting paranoid about fines and officials last season?

McCloskey: I think if you stay with it too long, or publicly talk about it too long, the guys become paranoid about the thing. Yeah, I think at the end of the year and the early part of the playoffs... I said to Bill and Rick on occasion that when they were fined for play, "You deserved that one." And also there have been times when I've said, "Hey, you didn't deserve that, and I will talk to Rod or someone in the league office about it."

Q: When he was a Piston, was Mahorn rougher?

McCloskey: I think he was rougher and more aggressive than most other players in the league. Oh sure.

Q: He was willing to push the limits?

McCloskey: Oh yeah. He's

Detroit was ready to celebrate its NBA title.

Jack lets Chuck do the coaching.

aggressive, and he's going to put a body on you when you're down inside. He is not afraid of body contact. And that is why we have officials.

Q: Do other general managers in the league call and raise hell with you ?

McCloskey: Oh sure. But, until we beat Boston, no one ever mentioned their names as being Bad Boys, or being mean. But, as soon as we started to win a little...

Q: Actually, your Bad Boys image was created for marketing?

McCloskey: That's correct.

Q: Did your efforts behind the scenes have to intensify because of this image?

McCloskey: I was trying to the point that we were going to downplay the image. You know, try and get it down. But, the thing just took off from

a marketing standpoint and hell, right now we'll let it ride its course.

Q: You really can't control the marketing?

McCloskey: No, that is the public. You can't fight that. The public will dictate that.

Q: Actually, the league put out the Bad Boys video, reinforcing that image. Do you remind the league of that?

McCloskey: The league has responsibility for that. The Bad Boys thing had its good points and bad points. The good part was that when teams played us, they often concentrated on our Bad Boys image rather than playing basketball.

The bad part was that officials became very, very cognizant of Mahorn and Laimbeer, who very often got into foul trouble while different individuals on another team

would commit the same crime, and the penalty would not be administered.

Then again, I can bring up guys on probably every team in the league... I can show tapes of a team out in the West that I'll tell ya, when you come off a screen, they pop you pretty good.

Q: Over the years, there has been a public perception that you and Chuck Daly don't always get along. Is there tension in your relationship?

McCloskey: I don't think we have any tension. I think years ago it was written that we didn't even talk, which was so erroneous. Also I think the fact he had situations involving his contract where the Sixers wanted him back, and I wasn't going to allow that unless we got a first-round pick as compensation. What it got down to is that we are not going to develop coaches for the 76ers or anybody else. Chuck and I have a great professional relationship.

Q: Do you ever have to tell yourself not to look over Chuck's shoulder?

McCloskey: It is good for me. I always say that I wouldn't want somebody coming to tell me that I did not do this or I didn't do that. I would really resent that. That is why I don't get involved in the coaching end at all. Occasionally, Chuck will come and ask me about this or that. And occasionally I will say something, but other than that, no. A coach has to be his own man. I'll talk to the assistants once in a while and say, "What do you think about this?" I'll ask about attacking the press, or about a player in the league.

The things they are doing are very positive. I think one of the things Chuck has done and also our assistants is that each guy has developed a role. It is formalized. They utilize each player's strength.

Q: Do you think this team has got everything?

McCloskey: I think this is a team the last three seasons that has had a chance to win the championship and this was the third shot at it. The first two we failed.

Q: Billy Packer describes you as very tough-minded, as tough as marine sergeant. Where does your tough mindedness come from?

McCloskey: Probably my parents. I grew up in a small coal mining community in eastern Pennsylvania, north of Philadelphia. It was a competitive athletic area. My father was a miner all his life; my mother was a very diligent, tough-minded woman.

Q: You were the only child in the family. Did you have a tough decision not to follow your father into the mines?

McCloskey: My father, when I was 14 or 15, said, "I am going to take you down one time, and it will be the last time. You're going to think about it.

because, you're going to go to school, get an education and you're going to have something better than I have." I went down with him, and that was a revelation. There was always a lot of water in the mines, and I remember his knees to his toes were always just raw. My mother would put Vaseline on his knees every morning with wax paper and then big socks on for him to go to work. My father died of black lung in 1974, and my mother is living in a nursing home in Pennsylvania.

Q: Your mom was the disciplinarian?

McCloskey: My dad never touched me, but my mom made sure I did things right. And if I didn't, I felt it or heard about it.

Q: Your generation faced the challenge of World War II. What were your experiences?

McCloskey: I was in the navy, eventually became a skipper of an LCT (a landing craft), made two invasions at Okinawa and Iwo Jima, the two northern most island we hit before Japan. I played some basketball occasionally over there. Our guys stole some plywood from the army, and we got a basket and put it up on the deck of the ship.

It was an exciting time. I was 19 at the time. I was on the beach when the great writer Ernie Pyle was killed. He was killed on Iwo Jima. I had met him, talked to him briefly. It sounds strange to talk like this about a war, but it was a great time when everybody was focused on one thing. It is like our team now, everybody is focused on the championship.

Q: In the past you've likened skippering the landing craft to coaching basketball.

McCloskey: We were sitting in Boston a few years back, the coaches and myself, a half hour before the game started. It was quiet in the locker room and I said, "This sounds ridiculous, but this is just like waiting to hit the beach when the battle ships bomb the beaches and then the planes hit it, and then it is your turn."

Q: The war shaped your whole generation.

McCloskey: Absolutely. I hear people and parents talk about their children, how they can't do this and can't do that, and I think, "They can all do it, if the circumstances merit it."

Q: What happened after the war?

McCloskey: I had been to school for two years and then was in the navy. I came back, and the day I came back, a couple of baseball teams came to visit me. The Tigers and the A's. I decided I was going to play professional baseball. But, I had to get down on my knees and swear to my mother that I would finish my education. I literally got down on my knees.

Q: You played pro basketball in the Eastern League. How did you get from pro baseball to the Eastern League?

McCloskey: I went back to school and played in the American League which was the forerunner of the NBA. Baltimore, Wilmington, Trenton, Paterson (NJ). We played in that area. When the NBA came in, it knocked some of those teams out. That is when I went to the Eastern League, while I was coaching in high school and going to school. The Eastern League was guys that just loved to play basketball. The money you got sometimes didn't pay for expenses. We used to have quite a team. Jack Ramsey, Stan Novak, and other guys. Most of them were coaching at the high school level. We would talk basketball to and from the games.

It was tough, rough, aggressive basketball. When you got hit, you really got hit. When you were a visitor, you usually got hit by a lady with an umbrella. Occasionally we would play an NBA team. We played mostly weekends. The teams were usually owned by some business man in town, an executive at the bank or somebody. Ramsey and I used to play for a furniture company and make a couple of bucks there. Once a week our team would practice.

Q: I believe you were the league's MVP?

McCloskey: I led the league in scoring two years, and I was MVP for two years.

Q: From there you moved into college coaching and eventually found your way to Wake Forest. How did you move from Wake Forest to the Portland Trailblazers?

McCloskey: The people at Portland were talking to me about a couple of my college players. At that time I had two offers to coach in the pros. The 76ers offered me the job there. And just about the time I was going to accept it, Harry Glickman talked to me about the Portland thing. And I thought the Portland thing was the most interesting.

Q: Even though you're from Pennsylvania?

McCloskey: Yeah, but at the same time, that was the year the 76ers only won nine games.

Q: Portland was an expansion team and had the number-one pick in the draft. Things seemed great, but they quickly went wrong?

McCloskey: When I got to Portland, they said that they were going to pick LaRou Martin. I had never heard of LaRou even being in college or heard of LaRou being an outstanding player, let alone being the number one player in the country.

They asked me who would you take and I said, "Bob McAdoo of the ACC." They brought McAdoo out and had an agreement with him and his agent that we were going to take McAdoo. We had the money all arranged. Then his agent asked for an additional $10,000 or 20,000 for himself, and the owner at that time said, "That's all off. We're not going to do it." So, that was how they got LaRou Martin.

Q: That has always been tagged as the classic case of an owner tampering in management?

McCloskey: Absolutely. That was catastrophic for the franchise and disastrous for us as new coaches.

Q: Is that the most painful experience you ever had in basketball?

McCloskey: Oh yeah. And it was painful for LaRou, because, first of all, I don't think he was expected to be picked in the first round, let alone the number one player in the country. He'll pass the buck that Neil Johnston and I didn't give him an opportunity to play. He really wasn't good enough. What we did was develop a guy by the name of Lloyd Neal, who became a very sound player on their championship team. Neil Johnston worked constantly with Lloyd Neal.

Q: The Portland years were hard?

McCloskey: We had a couple of guys, Sidney Wicks and Geoff Petrie, who didn't get along. It was a constant battle trying to get them to try and work together.

Q: After things turned sour in Portland, you became an assistant in Los Angeles?

McCloskey: I didn't go directly to L.A.; I went to Antigua. A friend of mine in Portland had an island off the mainland of Antigua, called Maria Antigua. It is now one of the most exclusive resort areas in the world. He asked me if I would be interested in helping him develop that. I jumped at the chance. Most of his money was tied up in the island. We worked with it for about a year. We dredged the harbor, could have put the Queen Mary in there. But the bottom fell out of the market, I think it was '74. That knocked the bottom out of us financially. Then Jerry West got the job with the Lakers, and I went to work in L.A.

Aguirre should be a factor this year.

Q: It must have been a very down time, with the economic failure and your experiences in Portland.

McCloskey: Absolutely. The Antigua thing was something that could have gone either way. You were going for the brass ring. It was great. It was like, you make a trade, you go for the big one, you go for the jugular. I could have been a millionaire in about a month, but it didn't work out. It was a great learning experience. A good business experience.

Q: Billy Packer said, "Jack is a coach first, last and always. I think Jack has a thorough understanding of all aspects of basketball, and the very least of that is business and administration. First Jack knew basketball and now he has added all these administrative abilities."

McCloskey: The coaching end was the only thing I was really interested in and thoroughly enjoyed. I can remember at Penn, the athletic director admonished me for an hour on not signing my middle initial on the awards certificates one year. So, that was one of the reasons I left Penn.

Q: Did you call Jerry West looking for a job after Antigua?

McCloskey: Yes, Pete Newell was also instrumental in that because he probably said to Jerry, "You should have an experienced person with you."

Q: Wasn't Jerry's back to the wall because the Lakers were rebuilding?

McCloskey: In fact, a year before we went there they had Kareem and didn't make the playoffs. The next year, the only player we added was a lame Don Chaney, and we had the best record in the league.

Q: Was it a good relationship with Jerry West?

McCloskey: I was there three years. I think we have a mutual respect.

Mahorn was a loss to the community as well as the team.

Q: Do you view it as a competition now with West (who manages the Lakers)?

McCloskey: Oh sure, but competition is not the right word to use. He said to me during the 1988 Finals, "If we don't win this, I am going to be so pleased if you do." And that is the way I feel about him. I don't think competition is the right word. If we were playing against each other, it would be competitive.

Q: Is this a fun job?
McCloskey: Very much so.

Q: As fun as coaching?

McCloskey: There is nothing better than winning from a coaching standpoint.

Q: What about playing?

McCloskey: I would love to be able to play with these guys, but now the court looks like a damn football field. Playing is the best when it's pure fun,

though. I think that's where players in this league begin to level off, when to them it becomes a job and not a game. In other words, when they say "Gee I got to go to practice again." There are guys like Vinnie Johnson who says, "Gosh, I'm going to practice again and have some fun." And he is at an age where he should be very limited, but he had a sensational year.

Q: Do you ever fantasize about going out there to play with the Bad Boys?

McCloskey: I would love to play. Some people say the old guys couldn't play with these guys. The only thing that is different is maybe leaping ability, because just playing the game, the older players could do very well.

Pistons
Profiles

MARK AGUIRRE

Position: Forward
Height: 6'6"
Weight: 232
High School: Chicago Westinghouse
College: DePaul '82
Birthdate: 12-10-59
When Drafted: First overall, Dallas 1981 as a hardship
How Acquired: Acquired from the Dallas Mavericks on February 15 in the NBA's biggest and most controversial trade of the season
Pro Experience: 8 Years
Married: Angela
Children: None
Residence: Chicago, IL

LAST SEASON: Acquired from the Dallas Mavericks on February 15 in the NBA's biggest and most controversial trade of the season...While acquiring Aguirre, the Pistons sent Adrian Dantley and Detroit's 1991 number-one draft choice to the Dallas Mavericks...Including the playoffs, the Pistons were 45-8 with Aguirre, sporting a 44-6 record when he was in the starting lineup...For the first time since his rookie campaign, he averaged less than 20 points per game...Entered the season with a career scoring average of 24.9 points per game, but in 1988-89 he averaged 18.9 points per game...With the Pistons, he finished the season by averaging 15.5 points per game...In 17 playoff games he averaged 12.6 points per game...All-time leading

scorer in Mavericks' history, averaged 21.6 points per game in 44 contests with Dallas...

AS A PRO: All-time leading scorer in Dallas Mavericks' history...Also the Mavericks' all-time leading rebounder and playoff scorer...Will surpass the 15,000 points scored total during the upcoming season...In 1984 was the first-ever Maverick to play in an All-Star Game...Has now played in three mid-season classics...Holds Maverick records for points in a quarter (24), a half (32), points in a game (49) and a season (2,330)...Was the first player selected in the 1981 NBA draft, while fellow Chicagoan and Pistons' team captain Isiah Thomas was the second player selected in that same college draft...

AS A COLLEGIAN: Led Depaul to a 79-10 record in his three years while averaging 24.5 points per game...Two-time consensus All-American...Received several player of the year honors during the post-season of his sophomore and junior seasons...Played in the Final Four as a freshman...Left Depaul after his junior season...Played on the 1980 United States Olympic Team...

PERSONAL: In 1988, married the former Angela Bowman on All-Star Saturday in Chicago, his hometown...Included in his wedding party were Isiah Thomas and Magic Johnson...Was cut the first time he tried out for his grade school team...Avid golfer who plays nearly every day during the off-season...

NBA CAREER RECORD

TEAM-YR	GP	MIN	FGM	FGA	PCT.	FTM	FTA	PCT	OFF	DEF	REB	AVE	AST	PF-DQ	ST	BL	PTS	AVE	HI
DAL.'82	51	1468	381	820	.465	168	247	.680	89	160	249	4.9	164	152- 0	37	22	955	18.7	42
DAL.'83	81	2784	767	1589	.483	429	589	.728	191	317	508	6.3	332	247- 5	80	26	1979	24.4	44
DAL.'84	79	2900	925	1765	.524	465	621	.749	161	308	469	5.9	358	246- 5	80	22	2330	29.5	46
DAL.'85	80	2699	794	1569	.506	440	580	.759	188	289	477	6.0	249	250- 3	60	24	2055	25.7	49
DAL.'86	74	2501	666	1327	.503	318	451	.705	177	268	445	6.0	339	229- 6	62	14	1670	22.6	42
DAL.'87	80	2663	787	1590	.495	429	557	.770	181	246	427	5.3	254	243- 4	84	30	2056	25.7	43
DAL.'88	77	2610	746	1571	.475	388	504	.770	182	252	434	5.6	278	223- 1	70	57	1932	25.1	38
DL-DT'89	80	2597	586	1270	.461	288	393	.733	146	240	386	4.8	278	229- 2	45	36	1511	18.9	41
TOTALS	602	20222	5652	11501	.491	2925	3942	.742	1315	2080	3395	5.6	2252	1819-26	518	231	14488	24.1	49

NBA HIGHS

	51	21	40		14	20		9	10	15		17		5	3	49		

3-POINT FIELD GOALS: 1981-82, 25-71 (.352); 1982-83, 16-76 (.211); 1983-84, 15-56 (.268); 1984-85, 27-85 (.318); 1985-86, 16-56 (.286); 1986-87, 53-150 (.353); 1987-88, 52-172 (.302); 1988-89, 51-174 (.293).
CAREER: 255-840 (.303).

NBA PLAYOFF RECORD

TEAM-YR	GP	MIN	FGM	FGA	PCT.	FTM	FTA	PCT	OFF	DEF	REB	AST	PF-DQ	ST	BL	PTS	AVE
DALL. '84	10	350	88	184	.478	44	57	.772	21	55	76	32	34- 2	5	5	220	22.0
DALL. '85	4	164	44	89	.494	27	32	.844	16	14	30	16	16- 1	3	0	116	29.0
DALL. '86	10	345	105	214	.491	35	55	.636	21	50	71	54	28- 1	9	0	247	24.7
DALL. '87	4	130	31	62	.500	23	30	.767	11	13	24	8	15- 1	8	0	85	21.3
DALL. '88	17	558	147	294	.500	60	86	.698	34	66	100	56	49- 0	14	9	367	21.6
DET. '89	17	462	89	182	.489	28	38	.737	26	49	75	28	38- 0	8	3	274	12.6
TOTALS	62	2,009	504	1,025	.492	217	298	.728	129	247	376	194	180- 5	47	17	1,309	20.1

3-POINT FIELD GOALS: 1983-84, 0-5; 1984-85, 1-2 (.500); 1985-86, 2-6 (.333); 1986-87, 0-4; 1987-88, 13-34 (.382); 1988-89, 8-29 (.276).
CAREER: 23-80 (.288).

NBA ALL-STAR RECORD

TEAM-YR	GP	MIN	FGM	FGA	PCT	FTM	FTA	PCT	OFF	DEF	REB	AST	PF-DQ	ST	BL	PTS	AVE
DALL '84	1	13	5	8	.625	3	4	.750	1	0	1	2	2- 0	1	1	13	13.0
DALL '87	1	17	3	6	.500	2	3	.667	1	1	2	1	1- 0	0	0	9	9.0
TOTALS	3	42	13	24	.542	8	10	.800	2	2	4	4	6- 0	2	1	36	12.0

JOE DUMARS

Position: Guard
Height: 6'3"
Weight: 195
College: McNeese State '85 (Business Management Major)
High School: Natchitoches-Central (LA)
Birthdate: 5/24/63
Birthplace: Natchitoches, LA
When Drafted: First Round (18th Overall) Detroit, 1985
How Acquired: College Draft
Pro Experience: Four Years
Marital Status: Married
Residence: Natchitoches, LA

LAST SEASON: No longer considered one of the league's most underrated guards...Named the Most Valuable Player in the 1989 NBA Finals, leading the World Champion Pistons with a 27.3 points per game average in the four-game sweep of the Lakers...Had by far his best season as a pro in 1988-89...Named to the NBA's First Team All Defense, joining teammate Dennis Rodman...Every year in the league he has improved his scoring average, increasing to 17.2 points per game during 1988-89...Shot a career best 51 percent from the field and 85 percent from the free-throw line...Scored his career high of 42 points on April 12 in Cleveland as Detroit clinched the Central Division title...In that game, he scored 24 points in the third quarter, tying the all-time club record for points in a quarter...Also, he scored 17 straight points, the second most consecutive points total scored in Pistons' history...For the first time in his career, he had a serious injury which sidelined him for an extended period of time...Broke his left hand versus New York on January 12 and had surgery two days later...Missed 12 straight games, but did return in just three weeks...Totaled 13 DNPs due to injury...

AS A PRO: His scoring average has increased each year he's been in the league...Averaged 9.4 points per game in his rookie campaign, then improved to 11.8 points in his second year, 14.1 points in his third year and 17.2 last year...After being inserted into the starting lineup during the middle of his rookie season, he has remained the team's starting off-guard since that time...Named to the NBA All-Rookie First Team in 1985-86...Had missed just three games in his first three NBA seasons, before breaking his hand last year...

AS A COLLEGIAN: Four-time All-Southland Conference selection...Southland Conference leading scorer in 1982, 1984 and 1985...Ranked sixth in the nation in scoring in 1984, averaging 26.4 points per game...All-time McNeese State scoring leader...Holds virtually every McNeese State scoring record...Finished his collegiate career with a 22.3 scoring average...Played in the 1984 U.S. Olympic Trials...Second-leading, all-time Southland Conference scoring leader behind Dwight Lamar...Still ranks among the nation's top 20 all-time leading scorers...

PERSONAL: Older brother David played pro football in the now defunct United States Football League...Comes from a football-oriented family...Has five brothers and one sister...In the 1984-85 McNeese State Media Guide, he listed his favorite athlete as the Pistons' Isiah Thomas...Married in September of 1989 to the former Debbie Nelson...Gave his NBA Championship ring to his father Joe II...

NBA CAREER RECORD

TEAM-YR	GP	MIN	FGM	FGA	PCT	FTM	FTA	PCT	OFF	DEF	REB	AVE	AST	PF-DQ	ST	BL	PTS	AVE	HI
DET.'86	82	1957	287	597	.481	190	238	.798	60	59	119	1.4	390	200-1	66	11	769	9.4	22
DET.'87	79	2439	369	749	.493	184	246	.748	50	117	167	2.1	352	194-1	83	5	931	11.8	24
DET.'88	82	2732	453	960	.472	251	308	.815	63	137	200	2.4	387	155-1	87	15	1161	14.1	25
DET.'89	69	2408	456	903	.505	260	306	.849	57	115	172	2.5	390	103-1	63	5	1186	17.2	42
TOTALS	312	9536	1565	3209	.488	885	1098	.806	230	428	658	2.1	1519	652-4	299	36	4047	13.0	42

NBA HIGHS

		53	18	24		14	16		5	6	8		14		5	2	42		

3-POINT FIELD GOALS: 1985-86, 5-16 (.313); 1986-87, 9-22 (.409); 1987-88, 4-19 (.210); 1988-89, 14-29 (.483).
CAREER: 32-86 (.372)

NBA PLAYOFF RECORD

TEAM-YR	GP	MIN	FGM	FGA	PCT	FTM	FTA	PCT	OFF	DEF	REB	AST	PF-DQ	ST	BL	PTS	AVE
DET.'86	4	147	25	41	.610	10	15	.667	6	7	13	25	16-0	4	0	60	15.0
DET.'87	15	473	78	145	.538	32	41	.780	8	11	19	72	126-0	12	1	190	12.7
DET.'88	23	804	113	247	.457	56	63	.889	18	32	50	112	50-1	13	2	284	12.3
DET.'89	17	620	106	233	.455	87	101	.861	11	33	44	96	31-0	12	1	300	17.6
TOTALS	59	2044	322	666	.483	185	220	.841	43	83	126	305	123-1	42	4	834	14.1

3-POINT FIELD GOALS: 1986-87, 2-3 (.667); 1987-88, 2-6 (.333); 1988-89, 1-12 (.083).
CAREER: 5-21 (.238)

James Edwards

Position: Center
Height: 7'1"
Weight: 252
College: Washington, '77
High School: Roosevelt, Seattle, WA
Birthdate: 11/22/55
Birthplace: Seattle, WA
When Drafted: Third Round (46th pick) Los Angeles, 1977
How Acquired: From Phoenix Suns in exchange for Ron Moore and Detroit's Second-Round Draft Choice in 1991
Pro Experience: 12 Years
Marital Status: Single
Residence: Phoenix, AZ

LAST SEASON: For the first time in his NBA career, he did not average in double figures...Averaged better than double figures in each of his first 11 seasons in the NBA and entered the year with a career scoring average of 15.0 points per game...In his first full season with the Pistons, he played in a total of 76 games, missing six games due to an ankle sprain...For the second straight playoff campaign, he made key contributions...Detroit has now played in the NBA Finals during both his campaigns in a Pistons' uniform...

AS A PRO: Acquired from the Phoenix Suns on February 24, 1988 in exchange for Ron Moore and a second-round draft choice...Played in 26 regular-season games with the Pistons that year...Averaged 5.4 points and 3.0 rebounds during the remainder of the season with the Pistons...Prior to that, he played in 43 games with Phoenix and averaged 15.5 points and 7.8 rebounds...Was a member of the Cleveland Cavaliers in 1981-82 when Chuck Daly was the coach...Ironically, at that time, Edwards was the starting center, while Bill Laimbeer was the backup...Eclipsed the 10,000 career point total during the 1987-88 campaign...Originally drafted by the Los Angeles Lakers in the 3rd round of the 1977 NBA Draft...

AS A COLLEGIAN: An All-Pac 8 performer at the University of Washington, finished as the school's second-leading all-time scorer with 1,548 points...Scored a collegiate high of 37 points in his junior year against Oregon State...Averaged 20.9 points and 10.4 rebounds as a senior...

PERSONAL: Makes his year-round home in West Bloomfield...Became heavily involved with several charities while in Phoenix and expects to do the same here in Detroit...He is a boating expert...

NBA CAREER RECORD

TEAM-YR	GP	MIN	FGM	FGA	PCT	FTM	FTA	PCT	OFF	DEF	REB	AVE	AST	PF-DQ	STE	BLO	PTS.	AVE
LA-IN.'78	83	2405	495	1093	.453	272	421	.646	197	418	615	7.4	85	322-12	53	78	1262	15.2
IND.'79	82	2546	534	1065	.501	298	441	.676	179	514	693	8.5	92	363-16	60	109	1366	16.7
IND.'80	82	2314	528	1032	.512	231	339	.681	179	399	578	7.0	127	324-12	55	104	1287	15.7
IND.'81	81	2375	511	1004	.509	244	347	.703	191	380	571	7.0	212	304-7	32	128	1266	15.6
CLV.'82	77	2539	528	1033	.511	232	339	.684	189	392	581	7.5	123	347-17	24	117	1288	16.7
CL-PH.'83	31	667	128	263	.487	69	108	.639	56	99	155	5.0	40	110-5	12	19	325	10.5
PHO.'84	72	1897	438	817	.536	183	254	.720	108	240	348	4.8	184	254-3	23	30	1059	14.7
PHO.'85	70	1787	384	766	.501	276	370	.746	95	292	387	5.5	153	237-5	26	52	1044	14.9
PHO.'86	52	1314	318	587	.542	212	302	.702	79	222	301	5.8	74	200-5	23	29	848	16.3
PHO.'87	14	304	57	110	.518	54	70	.771	20	40	60	4.3	19	42-1	6	7	168	12.0
DET.'89	76	1254	211	422	.500	133	194	.685	68	163	231	3.0	49	226-1	11	31	555	7.3
TOTALS	789	21107	4434	8835	.502	2414	3506	.689	1480	3452	4932	6.3	1236	2945-86	341	741	11282	14.3

NBA HIGHS

	GP	MIN	FGM	FGA									AST				BLO	PTS.
	16	29	18	19									18		7		7	39

3-POINT FIELD GOALS: 1979-80, 0-1 (.000); 1980-81, 0-3 (.000); 1981-82, 0-4 (.000); 1983-84, 0-1 (.000); 1984-85, 0-3 (.000); 1987-88, 0-1 (.000); 1988-89, 0-2 (.000). CAREER: 0-15 (.000)

NBA PLAYOFF RECORD

TEAM-YR	GP	MIN	FGM	FGA	PCT	FTM	FTA	PCT	OFF	DEF	REB	AST	PF-DQ	ST	BL	PTS	AVE
IND.'81	2	56	7	24	.292	0	0	.000	4	10	14	5	8-0	1	1	14	7.0
PHO.'83	3	7	11	26	.423	6	6	1.000	6	12	18	4	7-0	1	1	28	9.3
PHO.'84	17	463	93	189	.492	48	68	.706	22	69	91	27	62-3	4	11	234	13.8
DET.'88	22	308	56	110	.509	27	41	.659	23	45	68	11	55-0	2	10	139	6.3
DET.'89	17	317	40	85	.471	40	51	.784	11	25	36	12	53-0	1	8	120	7.1
TOTALS	61	1198	207	434	.477	121	166	.729	66	161	227	59	183-3	9	31	535	8.8

3-POINT FIELD GOALS: 1987-88, 0-1 (.000); 1988-89, 0-1. CAREER: 0-2 (.000).

106

VINNIE JOHNSON

Position: Guard
Height: 6'2"
Weight: 200
College: Baylor '79 (Education Major)
High School: F.D. Roosevelt (Brooklyn, NY)
Birthdate: 9/1/56
Birthplace: Brooklyn, NY
When Drafted: First Round (7th Overall) Seattle, 1979
How Acquired: In Exchange for Greg Kelser, Nov. 21, 1981
Pro Experience: 10 Years
Nickname: V.J.
Marital Status: Single
Residence: Southfield, MI

LAST SEASON: After struggling during the early portion of the season, he returned to his old form and had an outstanding final portion of the regular season and playoffs...Averaged 17.0 points per game during the four-game sweep of the Lakers in the NBA Finals...Over the final 59 games of the regular season, he averaged 15.8 points per game...For the seventh straight season, he averaged better than double figures...Played in every regular season game, joining only Dennis Rodman...While he again was the third guard in Chuck Daly's three-guard rotation, he did start 21 games...When he was a starter, the Pistons were 16-5...Had one of his best performances in the pros versus Utah on March 1 when he scored 34 points...In that game, he set the all-time Pistons' record for consecutive points scored when the "Microwave" heated up for 19 straight points at the end of the first half...

AS A PRO: Ranks on many of the Pistons' top 10 categories of all-time career leaders including points, steals and games played...Had probably his best season as a pro during the 1986-87 season when he was runner-up in the balloting for the NBA's Sixth Man Award...For most of the past four seasons, he has joined Dumars and Thomas in Coach Chuck Daly's three-guard rotation...Acquired by the Pistons on November 21, 1981 from the Seattle SuperSonics in exchange for Gregory Kelser...Had one strong season in Seattle in 1980-81 when he started 63 games as Gus Williams sat the year out...Was the NBA's top offensive rebounder in that season, averaging 2.4 offensive boards per game...

AS A COLLEGIAN: Played at Baylor after transferring from McLennon Junior College in Waco, Texas after his sophomore season...Was the Southwest Conference leading scorer his senior season, averaging 25.2 points per game...During his two-year stay at Baylor, he was named to the Associated Press' All-American Second Team twice and became the school's second all-time leading scorer...

PERSONAL: Was dubbed the "Microwave" by former Celtic and current King Danny Ainge a few seasons ago, because V.J. heats up in a hurry...Vinnie is the middle child of four brothers and three sisters...His younger brother Eric is in his senior season at Nebraska after transferring out of Baylor...Makes his year-round home in Southfield...

NBA CAREER RECORD

TEAM-YR	GP	MIN	FGM	FGA	PCT	FTM	FTA	PCT	OFF	DEF	REBS	AVE	AST	PF-DQ	ST	BLO	PTS	AVE	HI
SEA.'80	38	325	45	115	.391	31	39	.795	19	36	55	1.4	54	40-0	19	4	121	3.2	12
SEA.'81	81	2311	419	785	.534	214	270	.793	193	173	366	4.5	341	198-0	78	20	1053	13.0	31
SE-D'82	74	1295	217	444	.489	107	142	.754	82	77	159	2.1	171	101-0	56	25	544	7.4	20
DET.'83	82	2511	520	1013	.513	245	315	.778	167	186	353	4.3	301	263-2	93	49	1296	15.8	33
DET.'84	82	1909	426	901	.473	207	275	.753	130	107	237	2.9	271	196-1	44	19	1063	13.0	28
DET.'85	82	2093	428	942	.454	190	247	.769	134	118	252	3.1	325	205-2	71	20	1051	12.8	28
DET.'86	79	1978	465	996	.467	165	214	.771	119	107	226	2.9	269	180-2	80	23	1097	13.9	35
DET.'87	78	2166	533	1154	.462	158	201	.786	123	134	257	3.3	300	159-0	92	16	1228	15.7	30
DET.'88	82	1935	425	959	.443	147	217	.677	90	141	231	2.8	267	164-0	58	18	1002	12.2	28
DET.'89	82	2073	462	996	.464	193	263	.734	109	146	255	3.1	242	155- 0	74	17	1130	13.8	34
TOTALS	760	18596	3940	8305	.474	1657	2183	.759	1166	1225	2391	3.1	2541	1661-7	665	211	9585	12.6	35

NBA HIGHS

	46	16		25		11	12		8	6	12		15		5	3	35	

3-POINT FIELD GOALS: 1979-80, 0-1 (.000); 1980-81, 1-5 (.200); 1981-82, 3-12 (.250); 1982-83, 11-40 (.275); 1983-84, 4-19 (.211); 1984-85, 5-27 (.185); 1985-86, 2-14 (.143); 1986-87, 4-14 (.286); 1987-88, 5-24 (.208); 1988-89, 13-44 (.295).
CAREER: 48-200 (.240).

NBA PLAYOFF RECORD

TEAM-YR	GP	MIN	FGM	FGA	PCT	FTM	FTA	PCT	OFF	DEF	REB	AST	PF-DQ	ST	BL	PTS	AVE
SEA.'80	5	12	1	3	.333	0	0	—	0	2	2	2	1-0	1	0	2	0.4
DET.'84	5	132	17	46	.370	17	19	.895	5	9	14	12	9-0	1	1	51	10.2
DET.'85	9	235	53	103	.515	22	28	.786	15	12	27	29	24-0	6	1	128	14.2
DET.'86	4	85	22	49	.449	7	13	.538	8	9	17	11	9-0	3	0	51	12.8
DET.'87	15	388	95	207	.459	31	36	.861	20	24	44	62	33-0	9	4	221	14.7
DET.'88	23	477	101	239	.423	33	50	.660	35	40	75	43	48-0	17	4	236	10.3
DET.'89	17	620	106	200	.455	87	101	.861	11	33	44	96	31-0	12	1	300	17.6
TOTALS	78	1701	380	847	.449	157	208	.755	99	96	224	202	176-0	41	13	928	11.9

3-POINT FIELD GOALS: 1984, 0-1 (.000); 1984-85, 0-3 (.000); 1985-86, 0-1 (.000); 1986-87, 0-2 (.000); 1987-88, 1-7 (.142).
CAREER: 11-38 (.289)..

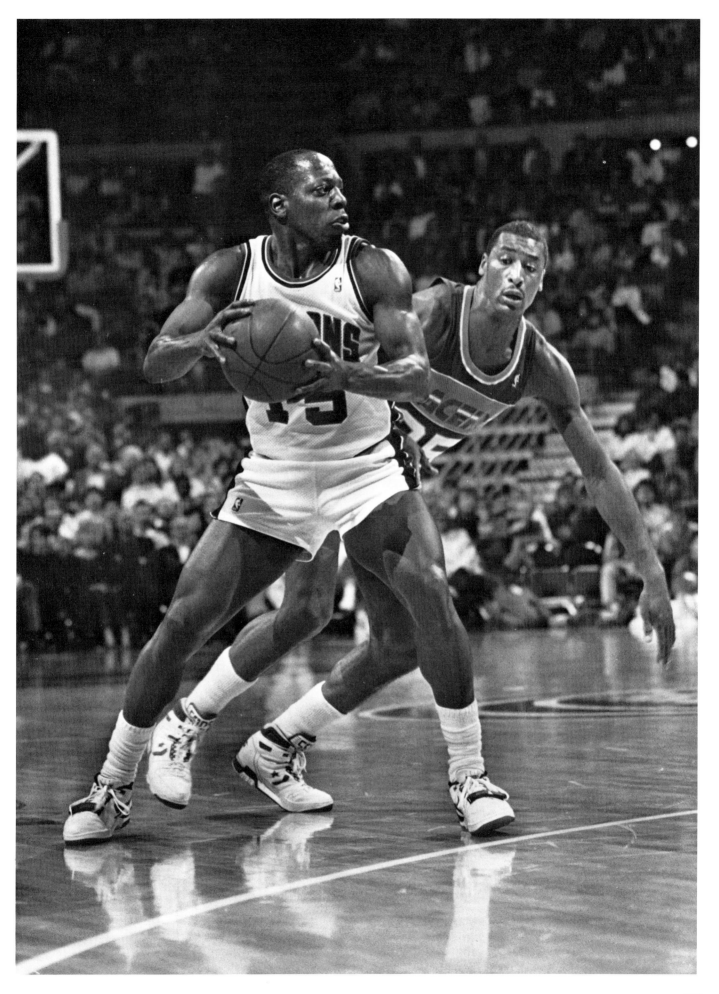

BILL LAIMBEER

Position: Center
Height: 6'11"
Weight: 245
College: Notre Dame (Degree in Economics)
High School: Palos Verdes, CA:
Birthdate: 5/19/57
Birthplace: Boston, MA
When Drafted: Third Round (65th Overall) Cleveland, 1979
How Acquired: From Cleveland with Kenny Carr for Phil Hubbard, Paul Mokeski, 1982 First Round Draft Choice, 1982 Second Round Draft Choice
Pro Experience: Nine Years
Nickname: Lambs
Married: Chris (1979)
Children: Eric William and Keriann
Residence: Orchard Lake, MI

LAST SEASON: Had his Iron Man streak snapped at 685 straight games played, fourth longest in NBA history...The streak came to a halt due to a league-imposed, one-game suspension after a fight with Cleveland's Brad Daugherty...Averaged better than double figures in rebounds in six straight seasons, before hauling down 9.6 rebounds per game in 1988-89...Twice during the year he grabbed 9 defensive rebounds in a quarter, an all-time Pistons' record...Has now averaged better than double figures in points in seven straight seasons...Went over the 10,000 career point total during the season...

AS A PRO: Has never missed an NBA game due to injury...During his nine-year NBA

career, he's missed one game due to Coach's Decision and one due to suspension...Ranks second on the Pistons all-time career rebound list trailing only Bob Lanier...Ranks in the top 10 of seven Pistons' all-time statistical categories...Came to the Pistons from Cleveland along with Kenny Carr in a deal that was made 9 minutes prior to the NBA trading deadline on Feb. 16, 1982...Started his first game with the Pistons and every one since...After not scoring 1,000 points in either of his first two NBA seasons, he's now surpassed 1,000 points in each of his last six seasons...Spent the 1979-80 in Italy (21 points per game) after being drafted by Cleveland in the third round of the 1979 NBA draft...Has been named to the NBA All-Star Team four times...Won the NBA rebounding title in 1985-86 when he averaged a career best 13.1 rebounds per game...

AS A COLLEGIAN: College teammate of former Piston Kelly Tripucka when the two were at Notre Dame...Made one appearance in the Final Four...As a senior at Notre Dame, his team was eliminated by eventual NCAA Champion Michigan State...

PERSONAL: High School All-American and two-time All-State pick in California...Played baseball and football in high school...In golf, has a one handicap and was the winner of the Cleveland Chapter of the NFL Alumni Association Golf Outing in 1982...Has organized the Bill Laimbeer 7-Eleven Muscular Dystrophy Golf Tournament each of the last six summers...Last summer, the event raised nearly $60,000 for MDA...Would love to play tournament golf when his playing days are complete...In June, 1984, he signed a contract that will keep him in Detroit through the 1990 season...He and his wife Chris are the parents of two children Eric and Keriann...

NBA CAREER RECORD

TEAM-YR	GP	MIN	FGM	FGA	PCT	FTM	FTA	PCT	OFF	DEF	REB	AVE	AST	PF-DQ	ST	BLO	PTS	AVE	HI
CLE.'81	81	2460	337	670	.503	117	153	.765	266	427	693	8.6	216	332-1	456	78	791	9.8	26
CL-D'82	80	1829	265	36	.494	184	232	.793	234	383	617	7.7	100	296-5	39	64	718	9.0	30
DET.'83	82	2871	436	877	.497	245	310	.790	282	711	993	12.1	263	320-9	51	118	1119	13.6	30
DET.'84	82	2864	553	1044	.530	316	365	.866	329	674	1003	12.2	149	273-4	49	84	1422	17.3	33
DET.'85	82	2892	595	1177	.506	244	306	.797	295	718	1013	12.4	154	308-4	69	71	1438	17.5	35
DET.'86	82	2891	545	1107	.492	266	319	.834	305	770	1075	13.1	146	291-4	59	65	1360	16.6	29
DET.'87	82	2854	506	1010	.501	245	274	.894	243	712	955	11.6	151	283-4	72	69	1263	15.4	30
DET.'88	82	2897	455	923	.493	187	214	.874	165	667	832	10.1	199	284-6	66	78	1110	13.5	30
DET.'89	81	2640	449	900	.499	178	212	.840	138	638	776	9.6	177	259-2	51	100	1106	13.6	32
TOTALS	734	24198	4141	8244	.502	1982	2385	.831	2257	5700	7957	10.8	1555	2647-52	512	727	10327	14.1	35

NBA HIGHS

	51	16	27		12	13		12	20	24		11		5	6	35		

3-POINT FIELD GOALS: 1980-81, 0-0 (.—); 1981-82, 4-13 (.308); 1982-83, 2-13 (.154); 1983-84, 0-11 (.000); 1984-85, 4-18 (.222); 1985-86, 4-14 (.286); 1986-87, 6-21 (.286); 1987-88, 13-39 (.333); 1988-89, 30-86 (.349). CAREER: 61-215 (.284).

NBA PLAYOFF RECORD

TEAM-YR	GP	MIN	FGM	FGA	PCT	FTM	FTA	PCT	OFF	DEF	REB	AST	PF-DQ	ST	BL	PTS	AVE
DET.'84	5	165	29	51	.569	18	20	.900	14	48	62	12	23-2	4	3	76	15.2
DET.'85	9	325	48	107	.449	36	51	.706	36	60	96	15	32-1	7	7	132	14.7
DET.'86	4	168	34	68	.500	21	23	.913	20	36	56	1	19-1	2	3	90	22.5
DET.'87	15	543	84	163	.515	15	24	.625	30	126	156	37	53-2	15	12	184	12.3
DET.'88	23	779	114	250	.456	40	45	.889	43	178	221	44	77-2	18	19	273	11.9
DET.'89	17	497	66	142	.465	25	31	.806	26	114	140	31	55-1	6	8	172	10.1
TOTALS	73	2477	375	781	.480	155	194	.799	169	562	731	140	259-9	52	52	927	12.7

3-POINT FIELD GOALS: 1984-85, 0-2 (.000); 1985-86, 1-1 (1.000); 1986-87, 1-5 (.200); 1987-88, 5-17 (.294). CAREER: 7-25 (.280).

NBA ALL-STAR RECORD

TEAM-YR	GP	MINS	AVE	FGM	FGA	PCT	FTM	FTA	PCT	OFF	DEF	REB	AVE	AST	PF-DQ	ST	BL	PTS	AVE
DET.'83	1	6	6.0	1	1	1.000	0	0	.—	1	0	1	1.0	0	1-0	0	0	2	2.0
DET.'84	1	17	17.0	6	8	.750	1	1	1.000	1	4	5	5.0	0	3-0	1	2	13	13.0
DET.'85	1	11	11.0	2	4	.500	1	2	.500	1	2	3	3.0	1	1-0	0	0	5	5.0
DET.'87	1	11	11.0	4	7	.571	0	0	.—	0	2	2	2.0	1	1-2	1	0	8	8.0
TOTALS	4	45	11.3	13	20	.650	2	3	.667	3	8	11	2.8	2	7-0	2	2	28	7.0

DENNIS RODMAN

Position: Forward
Height: 6'8"
Weight: 210
College: Southeastern Oklahoma State '86
High School: South Oak Cliff HS (TX)
Birthdate: 05/13/61
Birthplace: Dallas, TX
When Drafted: Second Round (27th Overall) Detroit, 1986
How Acquired: College Draft
Pro Experience: Three Years
Nickname: Worm
Marital Status: Single
Residence: Dallas, TX

LAST SEASON: Finished the season as the league's top field-goal percentage shooter, connecting on .595 of his attempts, shattering the all-time Pistons' record in the process...Was a NBA First Team All Defense selection...In fact, he missed being the only unanimous selection by just one vote...Finished second in the balloting for both the NBA's Defensive Player of the Year and the Sixth Man Award...Only NBA non-starter to grab more than 300 offensive rebounds...Improved his free-throw shooting to a career best 63 percent...One of the few NBA players to grab more rebounds (772) than he scored points (735)...Had his best game as a pro in Golden State on February 18 when he scored 32 points and grabbed 21 rebounds, both career highs...

AS A PRO: Has established himself as one of the NBA's top sixth men and offensive rebounders...Defensively, Coach Chuck Daly uses him at four positions...Has played in every game over the last two seasons...Entered the NBA from little-known Southeastern Oklahoma State and made an impact with the Pistons immediately...Has been used at both forward positions, and at big guard...Connecting on nearly 57 percent of his field-goal attempts in his first three NBA seasons...For the fourth straight off-season, he played on the Pistons Summer League Team...Nicknamed Worm, he suddenly became a Pistons fan favorite during his first year with the club...Has used Northwood Institute Coach Pat Miller as a shooting instructor over the past two seasons...

AS A COLLEGIAN: First Team NAIA All-American for three consecutive seasons...Did not play high school basketball and stood only 5'11" after his senior year...After graduation from high school, he grew 7 inches...Played one semester at Cooke County Junior College before transferring...Had 24 points and 19 rebounds in his first collegiate game, then followed with 40 points in his second game...As a sophomore, he scored 42 points and grabbed 24 rebounds in the semi-finals of the District Nine playoffs...Scored a career high of 51 points against Bethany Nazarene in the playoffs...

PERSONAL: His two sisters, Debra and Kim, were High School All-Americans and led South Oak Cliff to two state titles...Debra, 6'3", went on to Louisiana Tech, played on a national championship team and was a three-time All-American...Kim was an All-American at Stephen F. Austin...Needless to say, his two sisters influenced him tremendously...An outstanding pinball player...Runs a very successful summer basketball camp...

NBA CAREER RECORD

TEAM-YR	GP	MIN	FGM	FGA	PCT	FTM	FTA	PCT.	OFF	DEF	REB	AVE	AST	PF-DQ	ST	BL	PTS	AVE	HI
DET.'87	77	1155	213	391	.545	74	126	.587	163	169	332	4.3	56	166-1	38	48	500	6.5	21
DET.'88	82	2147	398	709	.561	152	284	.535	318	397	715	8.7	110	273-5	75	45	953	11.6	30
DET.'89	82	2208	316	531	.595	97	155	.626	327	445	772	9.4	99	292- 4	55	76	735	9.0	32
TOTALS	241	5510	927	1631	.568	323	565	.572	808	1011	1819	7.5	265	731-10	168	169	2188	9.1	32

NBA HIGHS

		42	13	17		9	11		10	13	21		5		4	4	32		

3-POINT FIELD GOALS: 1986-87, 0-1 (.000); 1987-88, 5-17 (.294); 1988-89, 6-26 (.231).
CAREER: 11-44 (.250).

NBA PLAYOFF RECORD

TEAM-YR	GP	MIN	FGM	FGA	PCT	FTM	FTA	PCT	OFF	DEF	REB	AST	PF-DQ	ST	BL	PTS	AVE
DET.'87	15	245	40	74	.541	18	32	.563	32	39	71	3	48-0	6	17	98	6.5
DET.'88	23	474	71	136	.522	22	54	.407	51	85	136	21	87-1	14	14	164	7.1
DET.'89	17	409	37	70	.529	24	35	.686	56	114	170	16	58-0	6	12	198	5.8
TOTALS	55	1128	148	280	.529	64	121	.533	139	238	377	40	193-1	26	43	460	6.5

3-POINT FIELD GOALS: 1987-88, 0-2 (.000); 1988-89, 0-4 (.000).
CAREER: 0-6 (.000).

JOHN SALLEY

Position: Forward/Center
Height: 6'11"
Weight: 231
College: Georgia Tech '86 (Degree in Industrial Management)
High School: Canarsie HS, Brooklyn, NY
Birthdate: 05/16/64
Birthplace: Brooklyn NY
When Drafted: First Round (11th Overall) Detroit, 1986
How Acquired: College Draft
Pro Experience: Three Years
Nickname: Spider
Marital Status: Single
Residence: Brooklyn, NY

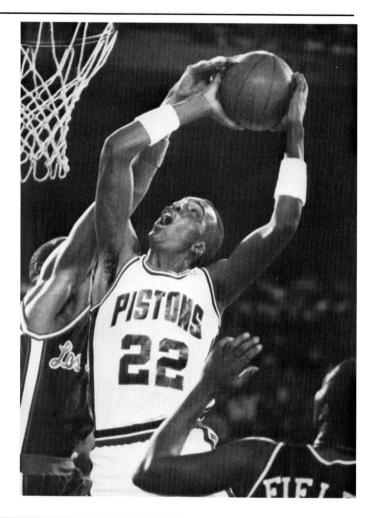

LAST SEASON: Played in a total of 67 games, starting 21 of those contests...He missed 15 straight games due to a broken bone in his left ankle...Those 15 misses were the first of his career, snapping his consecutive games played streak at 213...Made a strong showing in the playoffs especially in the early rounds...Had his best series against the Bucks in a four-game sweep when he averaged 13.5 points per game...During the regular season, he averaged 7.0 points and shot a career low .498 from the field...

AS A PRO: Started slowly in his rookie campaign, but has proved to be very consistent since that time...Has already recorded 334 blocked shots in his first three campaigns, which ranks him fourth on the all-time Pistons' blocked shots list...Had his best game as a pro during his rookie season when he scored 28 points, adding 10 rebounds and 5 blocked shots versus the Milwaukee Bucks on April 5, 1987...Set an all-time Pistons' playoff record with 10 offensive rebounds versus the Washington Bullets in the first round of the 1988 playoffs...

AS A COLLEGIAN: Finished fourth on the all-time Georgia Tech scoring list with 1,587 points (12.7 points per game), third in all-time FG percentage (.587) and is the school's all-time shotblocker (243)...Started 27 games as a freshman and averaged 11.5 points and 5.7 rebounds per game...Had a career high of 28 points against Monmouth on 1-17-85...Set a school record in his junior season when he connected on .627 of his field goal attempts...

PERSONAL: One of the most outgoing and personable players on the Pistons roster...Makes numerous personal appearances on behalf of the club throughout the year...Entered Georgia Tech as a 6-9, 185-pound forward and continued to add both size and strength...His nickname is Spider because of his long arms...Strengths are quickness, passing and shotblocking...Received his degree from Georgia Tech in the August of 1988...Runs a summer basketball camp...Aspiring comedian who makes appearances and comedy clubs during the year...His personal friends include Eddie Murphy and Spike Lee...

NBA CAREER RECORD

TEAM-YR	GP	MIN	FGM	FGA	PCT	FTM	FTA	PCT	OFF	DEF	REB	AVE	AST	PF-DQ	ST	BL	PTS	AVE	HI
DET.'87	82	1463	163	290	.562	105	171	.614	108	188	296	3.6	54	256- 5	44	125	431	5.3	28
DET.'88	82	2003	258	456	.566	185	261	.709	166	241	402	4.9	113	294- 4	53	137	701	8.5	19
DET.'89	67	1458	166	333	.498	135	195	.692	134	201	335	5	75	197- 3	40	72	467	7	19
TOTALS	231	4924	587	1079	.544	425	627	.678	408	630	1033	4.5	242	747-12	137	334	1599	6.9	28

NBA HIGHS

		40	10	15		8	10		7	8	11		4		3	5	28		

3-POINT FIELD GOALS: 1986-87, 0-1 (.000); 1988-89, 0-2 (.000).
CAREER: 0-3 (.000)

NBA PLAYOFF RECORD

TEAM-YR	GP	MINS	FGM	FGA	PCT	FTM	FTA	PCT	OFF	DEF	REB	AST	PF-DQ	ST	BL	PTS.	AVE
DET.'87	15	311	33	66	.500	27	42	.643	30	42	72	11	60-1	3	17	93	6.2
DET.'88	23	623	56	104	.538	49	69	.710	64	91	155	21	88-2	15	37	161	7.0
DET.'89	17	392	58	99	.586	36	54	.667	34	45	79	9	56-0	9	25	152	8.9
TOTALS	55	1326	147	269	.546	112	165	.679	128	178	306	41	206-3	27	79	406	7.4

3-POINT FIELD GOALS: 1987-88, 0-1 (.000); 1988-89, 0-1 (.000).
CAREER: 0-1 (.000).

ISIAH THOMAS

Position: Guard
Height: 6'1"
Weight: 185
College: Indiana University '83 (Criminal Justice Degree)
High School: St. Joseph (Westchester, IL)
Birthdate: 4/30/61
Birthplace: Chicago, IL
When Drafted: First Round (2nd Overall) Detroit, 1981
How Acquired: College Draft
Pro Experience: Seven Years
Married: Lynn
Children: Joshua
Residence: Bloomfield Hills, MI

Last Season: Had another All-Star season...Named to his 7th straight NBA All-Star Game, his sixth as a starter...Finished the regular season by averaging 19.5 points and 8.4 assists per game...Improved his shooting percentage to 46 percent after starting the season at 43 percent...Had another eventful playoff campaign leading the Pistons in scoring...Scored a playoff career high of 43 points in Game 6 of the NBA Finals versus the Lakers despite spraining his ankle early in the match. Was very limited in the decisive Game 7 and played very little in the final half of the final game due to the sprained right ankle...He averaged less than 20 points per game during the regular season.for only the second time in his career...For only the third time in his seven NBA seasons, he played less than 3,000 minutes...For the sixth straight season, he passed for more than 600 assists...Missed just one game during the 1987-88 campaign, and remains one of the league's most durable guards, missing just nine games over the last six seasons...

As A Pro: Has been named to the NBA All-Star Team in each of his first seven seasons in the league...Two-time All-Star Game Most Valuable Player, winning the honor in 1984 and 1986...First was MVP in Denver in 1984 when he scored 21 points and added 15 assists...Then in 1986 in Dallas, he scored 30 points, adding

10 assists and 5 steals to gain the honor...All-time Pistons leader in steals and assists, ranks third on the all-time Pistons scoring list...Set the an NBA record for assists in a single season (since broken by John Stockton) when he recorded 1,123 in 1984-85 for an average of 13.9 per game...Owns the Pistons' record for consecutive field goals made with 13...Has had some memorable playoff performances in leading the Pistons to five straight post-season appearances...Scored 25 points in the 3rd quarter of Game 6 versus the Lakers in the 1988 NBA Finals while playing with that sprained ankle, setting a record for points in a quarter in a Finals' game...Had 24 points in the 3rd quarter versus the Atlanta Hawks in the 1987 playoffs...Perhaps his most memorable playoff performance was in 1984 versus the New York Knicks when he scored 16 points in 94 seconds in the fourth quarter of the decisive Game 5 of that series...Was drafted by the Pistons second overall in the 1981 NBA College Draft after leaving Indiana after his sophomore season...

As A Collegian: Helped lead the Indiana Hoosiers to a 47-17 mark and an NCAA Championship (1981) with two Big Ten titles in his two seasons there...Missed only one game during his collegiate career and started all 63 games he played...All Big Ten as a sophomore...Was a consensus All-American after his sophomore season at Indiana...Top college scoring effort was 39 points versus the University of Michigan...Won 1981 NCAA Tournament Most Outstanding Player Award with 91 points in five games (18.2 points per game)...Member of the 1979 Pan-American Games Gold Medal Team, scoring 21 points in the title game, while leading the team in assists...Starter on the 1981 USA Olympic Team which had a 5-1 record against NBA All-Star Teams...

Personal: His wife, the former Lynn Kendall, gave birth to the couple's first child (Joshua Isiah) during the 1988 NBA Finals...Signed a contract on March 12, 1984, which will keep him in Detroit for the remainder of his basketball playing career...Youngest of nine children... One of the league's most vocal players in the fight against drug abuse, has made a 12-minute film entitled "Just Say No"...Received his degree in Criminal Justice in August of 1987.

NBA CAREER RECORD

TEAM-YR	GP	MIN	FGM	FGA	PCT	FTM	FTA	PCT	OFF	DEF	REB	AVE	AST	PF-DQ	ST	BLO	PTS	AVE	HI
DET.'82	72	2433	453	1068	.424	302	429	.704	57	152	209	2.9	565	253-2	150	17	1225	17.0	34
DET.'83	81	3093	725	1537	.472	368	518	.710	105	223	328	4.0	634	318-8	199	29	1854	22.9	46
DET.'84	82	3007	669	1448	.462	388	529	.733	103	224	327	4.0	914	324-8	204	33	1748	21.3	47
DET.'85	81	3089	646	1410	.458	399	493	.809	114	247	361	4.5	1123	288-8	187	25	1720	21.2	38
DET.'86	77	2790	609	1248	.488	365	462	.790	83	194	277	3.6	830	245-9	171	20	1609	20.9	39
DET.'87	81	3013	626	1353	.463	400	521	.768	82	237	319	3.9	813	251-5	153	20	1671	20.6	36
DET.'88	81	2927	621	1341	.463	305	394	.774	64	214	278	3.4	678	217-0	141	17	1577	19.5	42
DET.'89	80	2924	569	1227	.464	287	351	.818	49	224	273	3.4	663	209-0	133	20	1458	18.2	37
TOTALS	635	23276	4918	10632	.463	2814	3697	.761	657	1715	2372	3.7	6220	2095-40	1338	181	12862	20.3	319

NBA HIGHS

		52	19	34		16	20		6	11	12		25		7	4	47		

3-POINT FIELD GOALS: 1981-82, 17-59 (.288); 1982-83, 36-125 (.288); 1983-84, 22-65 (.338); 1984-85, 29-113 (.257); 1985-86, 26-84 (.310); 1986-87, 19-98 (.194); 1987-88, 30-97 (.309); 1988-89, 33-121 (.273).
CAREER: 212-762 (.278)

NBA PLAYOFF RECORD

TEAM-YR	GP	MIN	FGM	FGA	PCT	FTM	FTA	PCT	OFF	DEF	REB	AST	PF-DQ	ST	BL	PTS	AVE
DET.'84	5	198	39	83	.470	27	35	.771	7	12	19	55	22-1	13	6	107	21.4
DET.'85	9	355	83	166	.500	47	62	.758	11	36	47	101	39-2	19	4	219	24.3
DET.'86	4	163	41	91	.451	24	36	.667	8	14	22	48	17-0	9	3	106	26.5
DET.'87	15	562	134	297	.451	83	110	.755	21	46	67	130	51-1	39	4	361	24.1
DET.'88	23	911	183	419	.437	125	151	.828	26	81	107	201	71-2	66	8	504	21.9
DET.'89	17	633	115	279	.412	71	96	.740	24	49	73	141	39-0	27	4	309	18.2
TOTALS	73	2822	595	1335	.446	377	490	.769	97	238	335	676	239-6	173	29	1606	22.0

3-POINT FIELD GOALS: 1983-84, 2-6 (.333); 1984-85, 6-15 (.400); 1985-86, 0-5 (.000); 1986-87, 10-33 (.303); 1987-88, 13-44 (.296).
CAREER: 31-103 (.301).

NBA ALL-STAR RECORD

TEAM-YR	GP	MIN	FGM	FGA	PCT	FTM	FTA	PCT	OFF	DEF	REB	AST	PF-DQ	ST	BL	PTS	AVE
DET.'82	1	17	5	7	.714	2	4	.500	1	0	1	4	1-0	3	0	12	12.0
DET.'83	1	29	9	14	.643	1	1	1.000	3	1	4	7	0-0	4	6	19	19.0
DET.'84	1	39	9	17	.529	3	3	1.000	2	3	5	15	4-0	4	0	21	21.0
DET.'85	1	25	9	14	.643	1	1	1.000	1	1	2	5	2-0	2	0	22	22.0
DET.'86	1	36	11	19	.579	8	9	.889	0	1	1	10	2-0	5	0	30	30.0
DET.'87	1	24	4	6	.667	8	9	.889	2	1	3	9	3-0	0	0	16	16.0
DET.'88	1	28	4	10	.400	0	0	.000	1	1	2	15	1-0	1	0	8	8.0
DET.'89	1	33	7	13	.538	4	6	.667	1	1	2	14	2-0	0	0	19	19.0
TOTALS	8	231	58	100	.580	27	33	.818	11	9	20	79	15-0	19	0	147	18.3

FENNIS DEMBO

Position: Forward-Guard
Height: 6'6"
Weight: 215
College: Wyoming '88
High School: Fox Tech High School, San Antonio, TX
Birthdate: 1/24/66
Birthplace: Mobile, Alabama
When Drafted: Second Round (30th Overall) Detroit, 1988
How Acquired: College Draft
Pro Experience: One Year
Marital Status: Single
Residence: San Antonio, TX

Last Season: Was on the cover of Sports Illustrated in the college basketball preview issue before his senior season...Had his best scoring season when he averaged 20.4 points per game...Ranked among the Western Athletic Conference leaders in virtually every department while leading Wyoming into the NCAA tournament...Was a consensus pre-season All-American before his senior campaign.

As A Collegian: Finished his career as Wyoming's all-time leading scorer (2,311) and rebounder (954), while he was second in assists (405)...Enjoyed an outstanding freshman campaign, averaging 13.5 points and 7.3 rebounds...Became one of the Western Athletic Conference's top players in his sophomore campaign posting averages of 17 points and 6.7 rebounds per game...In his sophomore season he helped lead Wyoming to the National Invitational Tournament Finals and was named to the All-NIT Team...Raised his averages to 20.3 points and 8.3 rebounds per game during his junior season, and was named the WAC Player of the Year...Had an outstanding NCAA Tournament in his junior season when he averaged 27 points per game while leading Wyoming to the field of 16...Played on the United States Pan-American Team in 1987.

Personal: A fierce competitor who is very emotional during the game...Resides in San Antonio.

NBA CAREER RECORD

TEAM-YR	GP	MIN	FGM	FGA	PCT	FTM	FTA	PCT	OFF	DEF	REB	AVE	AST	PF-DQ	STE	BLO	PTS	AVE	HI
DET.'89	31	74	14	42	.333	8	10	.800	8	15	2.3	0.7	5	15- 0	1	7	36	1.2	8

3-POINT FIELD GOALS:1988-89, 0-4 (.000).

SCOTT HASTINGS

Position: Forward/Center
Height: 6'11"
Weight: 245
College: '82 Arkansas (Public Relations)
High School: Independence High School (KS)
Birthdate: 6/3/60
Birthplace: Independence, KS
When Drafted: New York, 1982 2nd round (29th overall)
How Acquired: Free Agent (Formerly with Miami Heat)
Pro Experience: 7 years
Married: Judy
Children: Ashley, Allison
Residence: Roswell, GA

LAST SEASON: Signed as an unrestricted free agent by the Pistons on July 17, 1989...Expected to play minutes at power forward position after the loss of Rick Mahorn to the expansion draft...Played for the expansion Miami Heat during the 1988-89 season, averaging 5.1 points per game in 75 appearances...He started six of those contests...

AS A PRO: Seven-year NBA veteran began his career with the New York Knicks...Traded during the middle of his rookie season and played the next five and one-half seasons with the Atlanta Hawks...Was then acquired by Miami in the 1988 NBA expansion draft...Original second-round draft choice of the Knicks (29th overall) in 1982...Traded along with $600,000 to Atlanta for Rory Sparrow in February of 1983...

AS A COLLEGIAN: Honorable mention All-American during his senior season at Arkansas...Left Arkansas as the second leading all-time scorer behind only Sidney Moncrief...Led Razorbacks in scoring during his sophomore, junior and senior seasons...

PERSONAL: Conducts his own basketball camp in Kansas during the off-season...Avid golfer...Also won high school letters in both tennis and football...Kansas Player-of-the-Year as a senior...Majored in Public Relations in college...Scott and wife Judy are parents of two daughters, Ashley and Allison...

NBA CAREER RECORD

TEAM-YR	GP	MIN	FGM	FGA	PCT	FTM	FTA	PCT	OFF	DEF	REB	AST	PF-DQ	STE	BLO	PTS.	AVE
NY-ATL'83	31	140	13	38	.342	11	20	.550	15	26	41	3	34- 0	6	1	37	1.2
ATL. '84	68	1135	111	237	.488	82	104	.788	96	174	270	46	220- 7	40	38	305	4.5
ATL. '85	64	825	89	188	.473	63	81	.778	59	100	159	46	135- 1	24	23	241	3.8
ATL. '86	62	650	65	159	.409	60	70	.857	44	80	124	26	118- 2	14	8	193	3.1
ATL. '87	40	256	23	68	.338	23	29	.783	16	54	70	13	35- 0	10	7	71	1.8
ATL. '88	55	403	40	82	.488	25	27	.926	27	70	97	16	67- 1	8	10	110	2.0
MIAMI'89	75	1206	143	328	.436	91	107	.850	72	159	231	59	203- 5	32	42	386	5.1
TOTALS	395	4615	484	1100		355	438		329	663	992	209		134	129	1343	

NBA HIGHS

41				9	10			17	6				3	3	17	

NBA PLAYOFF RECORD

TEAM-YR	GP	MIN	FGM	FGA	PCT	FTM	FTA	PCT	OFF	DEF	REB	AST	PF-DQ	STE	BLO	PTS	AVE
ATL.'84	5	32	2	9	.222	3	4	.750	2	6	8	1	4-0	1	0	7	1.4
ATL.'86	9	49	11	14	.786	5	11	.455	3	7	10	2	11-0	2	0	28	3.1
ATL.'87	4	21	2	3	.667	2	2	1.000	1	5	6	0	5-0	1	1	6	1.5
ATL.'88	11	103	9	14	.643	8	8	1.000	7	10	17	3	21-1	3	1	26	2.4
TOTALS	29	205	24	40	.600	18	25	.720	13	28	41	6	41-1	7	2	67	2.3

PLAYOFF HIGHS

	4	5		4	5		2	3	4			1		2	0	10

ANTHONY COOK

Position: Forward
Height: 6'9"
Weight: 190
High School: Van Nuys, CA
Birthdate: 5/19/67
Birthplace: Los Angeles, CA
How Acquired: Trade for Kenny Battle and Michael Williams
Experience: Rookie
Marital Status: Single
Residence: Los Angeles, CA

LAST SEASON: The Pistons acquired his rights on draft day from the Phoenix Suns in exchange for Michael Williams and the rights to Kenny Battle... Did not participate with the Pisonts' entry in the California Summer Pro League... All Pac 10 performer in both 1988 and 1989... Scored a career best 17.7 points in his final season at Arizona... Set school record with 80 blocked shots in his senior season... Fourth leading scorer in Arizona history and third leading rebounder...

AS A COLLEGIAN: The Pac 10's all-time career shot blocker... Led the Wildcats in rebounding during each of his final two seasons at Arizona... Scored his career high of 31 points versus USC during his senior season... During his four-year career, he started 122 of 132 games...

PERSONAL: Sociology major... Product of Van Nuys High School in California... Hometown is Los Angeles...

COLLEGE CAREER RECORD

YEAR	GP	FGM	FGA	PCT	FTM	FTA	PCT	REB	AST	PTS	AVE
'86	32	73	146	.500	48	73	.658	137	41	194	6.1
'87	30	118	246	.480	54	100	.540	217	18	290	9.7
'88	38	201	325	.618	126	176	.716	269	15	528	13.9
'89	33	237	377	.629	104	166	.627	238	12	578	17.5
TOTALS	133	629	1094	.576	332	515	.645	861	86	1590	12.0

MARK HUGHES

Position: Center/Forward
Height: 6'8"
Weight: 235
High School: Reeths Puffer High School (Muskegon, MI)
Birthdate: 10/5/66
Birthplace: Muskegon, MI
How Acquired: Free Agent
Experience: Rookie
Marital Status: Single
Residence: Muskegon, MI

LAST SEASON: Co-captained the 1989 NCAA Champion Michigan Wolverines...Averaged 6.8 points and 4.1 rebounds for the Wolverines during his senior season...Signed as a free agent in July of 1989...After not being selected in the June draft, he was invited to participate in the Pistons' Free Agent Camp in July...After impressing the Pistons' coaching staff in the California Summer Pro League, he was signed to a contract and invited to Veteran Camp in October...

AS A COLLEGIAN: Four-year performer at the University of Michigan...After starting 47 games in his sophomore and junior seasons, he started just four contests in his final campaign...Scored his career high of 17 points versus Purdue in his senior season...Missed the second half of his freshman season due to arthroscopic knee surgery...

PERSONAL: High school product of Muskegon Reeths Puffer...Led Reeths Puffer to semi-finals of the state tournament in his senior season...Sociology major at Michigan...

COLLEGE CAREER RECORD

YEAR	GP	FGM	FGA	PCT	FTM	FTA	PCT	REB	AST	PTS	AVE
UofM '86	14	12	24	.500	7	9	.778	18	2	31	2.2
UofM '87	32	86	158	.544	22	29	.759	192	42	194	6.1
UofM '88	34	65	123	.526	26	43	.605	133	33	156	4.6
TOTALS	80	163	305	.534	55	81	.679	343	77	381	4.8

WILLIAM DAVIDSON

MANAGING PARTNER

After 15 long years, Pistons' Managing Partner William Davidson achieved his ultimate goal: A World Championship for his team.

Detroit's 1989 World Championship can be directly attributed to Davidson, the club's majority owner since 1974. Under Davidson's direction, the Pistons have been considered one of the league's elite franchises for three years.

Now, after Detroit won its first-ever NBA Championship, never in the history of the franchise has the future looked brighter. In 1988-89, the Pistons began play in The Palace of Auburn Hills, a state-of-the-art arena built with Davidson's financial support. The Pistons are coming off the three most successful seasons in the history of the franchise.

For the second straight season, the Pistons advanced to The NBA Finals, and after finishing second in 1988, Davidson's accomplished the ultimate in 1989, a first-ever NBA Championship. The Pistons have now won the Central Division in each of the last two seasons, including a club record 63-19 record in 1988-89. Including the playoffs, the Pistons were 78-21 for the year, recording one of the single-most successful seasons in the history of the NBA.

Davidson acquired the Detroit Pistons in 1974 from the late Fred Zollner, the man who founded the team in Fort Wayne in the 1940s and moved the franchise to Detroit in 1957-58.

Interested in a wide variety of sports, Davidson is one of the most knowledgeable heads of an NBA franchise. He has studied the talents and abilities of players and coaches in the league and has some very astute observations.

The Pistons' majority owner likes success and has known it in his business interests. That's why now, the success of the Detroit Pistons comes as no surprise to those who are aware of Davidson's ability to manage people.

Educated in Business and Law, Davidson received a Bachelor's Degree in Business Administration from the University of Michigan and earned a Juris Doctor's Degree from Wayne State University.

After three years, Davidson gave up his law practice to take over a wholesale drug company, rescued it from bankruptcy and turned it around in three years. Then, he took over a surgical supply company which was on the verge of bankruptcy and saved it as well. The next step was to take the Guardian Glass Company, the family business, turning it around in two years by paying off all debts and heading it on a profitable growth path which the company enjoys now. Even today, Guardian Industries remains the flagship of his business interests.

Davidson expects his previous track record to help pave the way for the Pistons and The Palace. The success he has enjoyed has come from a proven talent for hiring competent managers and placing the responsibility with them. That is the same formula he has used with the Detroit Pistons for the past 14 years and now expects to do the same with an arena he believes will be one of the best in the world.

The athletic interests of Davidson date back many years

and have continued alongside his business career. He was a high school and college track man and played freshman football in the Navy during World War II. Davidson was an initial inductee into the Jewish Sports Hall of Fame.

Davidson's management talents are continually on display in NBA circles, where he is active on the player relations and finance committees. He was a member of the committee which selected former NBA Commissioner Lawrence O'Brien in 1975. Davidson, who can usually be found sitting courtside at most Pistons' home games, is active in numerous community and charitable affairs.

The Detroit Pistons ownership group includes Legal Counsel Oscar Feldman, and Advisory Board Members Warren Coville, Ted Ewald, Milt Dresner, Bud Gerson, Dorothy Gerson, David Mondry, Eugene Mondry, Ann Newman, Herb Tyner and William Wetsman.

Jack McCloskey
GENERAL MANAGER

Jack McCloskey enters his 11th season as the General Manager of the Detroit Pistons. The Pistons' 1989 NBA World Championship is a direct result of his endless hours of hard work. Through the NBA draft and many shrewd trades, McCloskey has built the Pistons into one of the elite franchises in the National Basketball Association.

Throughout the NBA, McCloskey has acquired the nickname "Trader Jack" because of his ability to swing a deal and then have the acquired player make an immediate impact upon the Pistons' team. In 1988-89, his acquiring of Mark Aguirre in mid-season only added to his reputation. After the trade, the Pistons finished with a 45-8 record on their way to a first-ever NBA Championship.

When the Pistons needed an astute basketball mind to direct the on-court fortunes of the club, Managing Partner William Davidson appointed NBA veteran McCloskey as General Manager on December 11, 1979. Over those past 10 years, McCloskey's trades have often been the talk of the league due to the success of the Pistons on the court.

At the time of the announcement of McCloskey as the team's General Manager, Davidson called the addition "a positive step in the building of our franchise to an NBA Championship level." After 10 hard years of work, McCloskey assembled the 1989 World Champions. Additionally, the Pistons are two-time Eastern Conference Champions and two-time Central Division Champions. Indeed, the Pistons have arrived as a Championship level basketball team.

In each of the last three seasons, McCloskey has been considered among the top executives in the NBA. With his ability to select top-notch collegiate talent through the NBA draft, McCloskey has been able to keep the Pistons at a championship level. In 1981-82, he was recognized by his peers as one of the league's top general managers when he was voted runnerup in the Sporting News' Executive of the Year balloting. In each succeeding season, McCloskey has been considered for the award.

McCloskey's duties include authority over all basketball-playing aspects of the Pistons organization including coaching, player personnel, all scouting and trades.

A native of Mahanoy City, PA, McCloskey came to the Pistons from the Indiana Pacers where he served as an assistant to head coach Bob Leonard during the 1979-80 season. Previously, he assisted Jerry West, now the general manager of the Los Angeles Lakers, for three seasons.

Upon joining the Pistons, McCloskey, a 1948 graduate of the University of Pennsylvania, had 23 years of coaching experience behind him. During his playing days, he was an acknowledged all-around athlete, playing basketball and football at Penn, plus eight years in the American and Eastern Basketball League. His career as a player also includes a brief stint in the NBA and four years of professional basketball in the Philadelphia A's organization. McCloskey and diminutive guard Charlie Criss rank as the Eastern League's only two-time MVP's. His Eastern League teammates included current Pistons' Director of Scouting

Stan Novak and former Indiana Pacers' Head Coach Jack Ramsay.

It was after a highly successful high school coaching career that McCloskey returned to Penn in 1956, inheriting a team that went from 7-19, then 13-12 and 12-14 before seven straight winning seasons with Ivy League first-division finishes annually. In his final season, McCloskey led the 1965-66 Penn team to a 19-6 campaign, the most wins since 1954-55, capturing the Ivy League title. His teams were 87-53 in Ivy League play and won the Philadelphia Big Five Title in 1963 on their way to an overall 146-105 record in 10 seasons.

McCloskey's next stop was Wake Forest, where he transformed the lowly Deacons into an Atlantic Coast Conference contender. After a 14-39 mark in his first two years, he followed with four successful seasons in the rugged ACC while compiling a 56-50 slate. His assistants were Billy Packer and the late Neil Johnston, former NBA scoring ace of the old Warriors.

His next chore was to take over the expansion Portland TrailBlazers in 1972-73 for two painful building seasons. The Pacific Division team was an eventual NBA champion. In his tenure with the Lakers, he served as the offensive coordinator for two seasons and defensive coordinator for a year as the Lakers bounced back from two losing seasons with three winning campaigns.

Jack and wife Leslie make their home in West Bloomfield. One of the top senior tennis players in the state, Jack was a 1981 inductee into the Jerry Wolman Chapter of the Pennsylvania Sports Hall of Fame.

Thomas S. Wilson

CHIEF EXECUTIVE OFFICER

Over the last six seasons, the Detroit Pistons have been one of the most successfully marketed franchises in the National Basketball Association. Not only has that been proven through five league-leading attendance marks and sellouts every night, but also by the current all-time high interest mark in the club. One of the major factors behind the financial success the Detroit Pistons now enjoy is Chief Executive Officer Thomas S. Wilson.

In 1988-89, when Detroit won its first-ever NBA Championship, the club sold out every home game and set both television rating records and merchandising sales marks for both the Pistons and the NBA.

Over the last 10 years with the Pistons, Wilson's duties and responsibilities have continued to increase dramatically. As the Pistons' chief executive officer, Wilson oversees all the administrative, marketing, broadcasting and promotional efforts of the organization.

Wilson's workload increased dramatically with the opening of The Palace of Auburn Hills in 1988. New home of the Detroit Pistons, the Palace was designed largely around Wilson's input. the Pistons have been able to customize the new facility to provide the finest sightlines and comfort levels for basketball of any arena in the country. Wilson took on the responsibility of staffing the arena and of developing the philosophies that will present all of the arena's events in the finest manner possible. Now, the state-of-the-art Palace has been cited as one of the best arenas in the world.

Wilson spent much of the previous three years traveling around the United States and Canada studying all aspects of various arenas and incorporating the best features of each into the Pistons' new home.

"The success of the Detroit Pistons has been very rewarding to the organization, to me personally, but the challenge of designing the finest facility ever built for basketball and other events has been the most exciting project I have been involved with.

"We began with the Pistons in the final season at Cobo, lived through the down season and shared the success of the current era, which culminated with a World Championship in 1989. I know our staff anxiously awaits the opportunity as we move into the brightest time in our history."

Wilson joined the Pistons in 1978 and watched the team linger through several poor seasons. After a 16-66 season, the Pistons' attendance figures dropped below 6,000 per game. But, when the team drafted Isiah Thomas in 1981 and made several other key acquisitions through trades and subsequent drafts, the future began to look much brighter.

Under Wilson's leadership, the Pistons have now led the NBA in attendance in each of the last five seasons. The Pistons set the all-time NBA record for attendance in 1987-88 becoming the first NBA franchise to attract one million fans during the regular season. By averaging 26,012 fans per game, the Pistons have established an NBA record that may never be broken.

The Pistons' outstanding success in broadcasting is also headed by Wilson. When the Pistons moved both the television and radio broadcast in-house he was responsible for overseeing all aspects. Over the last two seasons, the Pistons have set franchise records in television ratings.

He continues to be involved with broadcasting as he serves as the color commentator for all Pistons' games on Pro-Am Sports Systems (PASS). In 1989-90, Wilson will team-up with Channel 4's Fred McLeod telecasting the games on cable.

A native Detroiter, Wilson received his bachelor's of business administration from Wayne State University. Prior to joining the Pistons, he worked for both the Los Angeles Lakers and the Los Angeles Kings, and the Forum. He also worked in films and television in California, appearing in over 40 television programs.

An inveterate runner, he has participated in two Detroit Free Press Marathons. Tom and his wife Linda reside in Rochester Hills with daughters Kasey and Brooke.

Chuck Daly

HEAD COACH

Directing the Detroit Pistons to the team's first-ever World Championship was the popular Coach Chuck Daly. In six seasons, Daly is the most successful coach in the history of the Detroit Pistons.

Under Daly's direction, the club has enjoyed its most successful years, capped off by the 1989 World Championship.With Daly directing from the sidelines, the club has recorded six straight winning seasons and six straight playoff appearances. Prior to his arrival, the club had never recorded back-to-back winning campaigns.

Daly made another strong bid for Coach of the Year honors after directing the Pistons to a 63-19 record in 1988-89. Then, in the playoffs the Pistons were 15-2, while winning the championship. Twice in 1988-89, Daly was named the NBA Coach of the Month, first in November and then again in March. During the month of March, the Pistons tied the NBA record for wins in a month, recording a sterling 16-1 mark.

The Pistons have enjoyed the top three seasons in the history of the franchise under his direction (1987-1988-1989). The Pistons are the two-time defending Eastern Conference Champions and the two-time defending Central Division Champions. Prior to that, the Pistons had never won a divisional title in 31 years in Detroit.

After tying the club record with 52 wins in 1986-87, the Pistons recorded a 54-28 mark in 1987-88. Then last season, the Pistons became one of the few NBA franchises to ever reach the 60-win plateau, finishing with a 63-19 record. Including the playoffs, Detroit was 78-21 last season under Daly. His six-year regular-season coaching record now stands at 310-182, easily making him the winningest coach in the history of the franchise. Daly's six-year playoff coaching record is 47-26 (64 percent), trailing only Pat Riley among active NBA coaches in playoff winning percentage.

In his first season with the Pistons in 1983-84, Daly improved the club by 12 games, as the Pistons finished with a 49-33 record. In the next two campaigns, the Pistons finished with 46-36 marks and post-season appearances. The Pistons then enjoyed the most successful seasons in the history of the franchise in Daly's fourth, fifth and sixth seasons with the club.

Daly was named the head coach of the Pistons on May 17, 1983. His more than 30 years of success at all levels of coaching easily carried over with the Pistons.

Prior to joining the Pistons, Daly spent four-plus seasons as an assistant to Billy Cunningham and the Philadelphia 76ers. The Sixers were 236-104 in regular-season play during those four-plus years, winning two division titles and finishing second twice. The Sixers also logged a 32-21 playoff record in the four seasons, before he departed for the Cleveland Cavaliers' head coaching position. Daly was regarded by the Sixers as especially adept at setting up offenses and defenses for various opponents.

In Daly's six seasons (1971-77) as the head coach of the University of Pennsylvania, his teams won four Ivy League titles and were runners-up twice. Penn won three Big Five Championships outright and tied for another under Daly's guidance, while compiling an overall record of 125-38 (.744 percentage) and won 20 of 25 Big Five games (.800 percentage). In his first season as the Penn head coach, he led the Quakers to a 25-3 record, a No. 3 ranking nationally and first place in the Eastern Collegiate Athletic Conference (ECAC). Daly led Penn to more NCAA berths and Big Five titles than any other head coach at Penn.

Daly was the head coach at Boston College for two seasons (1969-71) with a 26-26 record. He had served as an assistant at Duke for seven years (1963-69), first as freshman coach and then four years as the varsity assistant coach.

A graduate of Bloomsburg University, after starting his collegiate career at St. Bonaventure, Daly earned a Master's Degree at Penn State and began his coaching career at Punxsutawney High School.

Daly, a native of Kane, Pennsylvania, has become a very popular speaker on the banquet circuit, and has numerous endorsements with sponsors. He is the host of the very popular television show Chuck Daly's One on One. Chuck, and his wife Terry reside in West Bloomfield. They have one daughter (Cydney), a Penn State graduate who works for Revlon.

Will Robinson

ADMINISTRATIVE ASSISTANT TO THE GENERAL MANAGER

Will Robinson has dedicated his life to basketball. Recently, the game has been returning the favor as the Robinson legacy continues.

In the spring of 1982, Will was inducted into the Michigan Sports Hall of Fame, the supreme honor in the state where he enjoyed most of his coaching success. That success has continued during his years with the Pistons where he currently is the team's director of community relations and the administrative assistant to General Manager Jack McCloskey. His duties include scouting, special assignments and working the Pistons' training camp.

The list of names of the athletes who played for Robinson reads like a Who's Who in sports. His teams were usually tagged with the title "Champion."

Robinson's Detroit Miller High School team, paced by the great Sammy Gee, won the city championship over St. Joseph's High School in 1947, drawing 16,249 to Olympia Stadium. The game turnout set a Michigan attendance mark that stood until the Pistons moved to the Pontiac Silverdome in 1978.

When Robinson moved to Detroit Pershing High School, the name changed but the results were the same as his teams continued rolling up championships, winning at an 85 percent clip.

In 1963, Pershing and the PSL returned to state tournament play, and the team went to the final four of the state tournament led by Mel Daniels (former ABA center), Ted Sizemore (major league baseball player) and Willie Iverson (ABL Miami Floridians.)

One of the strongest high school basketball teams ever asembled played for Robinson in 1967. The five all later played in professional sports. Spencer Haywood and Ralph Simpson (both NBA and ABA), Glen Doughty and Paul Seals (pro football) and Marvin Lane (major league baseball) won the state championship.

The Robinson name soon was recognized nationally, and Illinois State Athletic Director Milt Weisbecker gave the coach a chance at the big-time collegiate game. Robinson became the first black coach to direct a major college team and recorded five consecutive winning seasons. Among his standouts were All-Pro guard Doug Collins, one of the many Olympians Robinsons produced, and Bubbles Hawkins, who later played guard with the New Jersey Nets.

There have been other standouts: Wayne State all-time great Charlie Primas, Baltimore Colt All-Pro Big Daddy Lipscomb, Wayne State VP Noah Brown, Olympians Lorenzo Wright and Charley Fonville and political advisor Ofield Dukes. The athletic field was not the only place where Robinson was developing outstanding individuals. He is just as proud of the 25 Detroit police officers who played for him, the college grads with Ph. D.s attached to their names and the sons of his players who are now headline-makers.

Robinson's induction into the Michigan Sports Hall of Fame marked the fifth such honor for him. He was previously tapped for the Michigan High School Coaches' Hall of Fame, the West Virginia State Hall of Fame, the Illinois State Hall of Fame and the Dapper Dan Hall of Fame.

Robinson, who makes his home in Detroit, has one son, William Jr., the coordinator of academic programs at the University of Michigan.

Robinson's induction into the Michigan Sports Hall of Fame marked the seventh such honor bestowed him. The others include: The Michigan High School Coaches Hall of Fame. The West Virginia State Hall of Fame, The Illinois State Hall of Fame, The Upper Ohio Valley Dapper Dan Hall of Fame, The Afro-American Sports Hall of Fame and the Michigan High School Basketball Hall of Fame.

Brendan Suhr

ASSISTANT COACH

Brendan Suhr, a ten-year veteran of the NBA, begins his first full season as top assistant for the 1989 World Champions. Suhr joined the Pistons in January of the 1988-89 season when then top assistant, Dick Versace, left to take over the head coaching duties of the Indiana Pacers. Suhr, considered a superb technician and teacher, will be on the bench for every game with duties that include practice and game coaching as well as scouting.

Before joining Chuck Daly's staff, Suhr served as assistant general manager and director of scouting for the Atlanta Hawks. He joined the Hawks in the 1979-80 season as an assistant coach and held that position for seven consecutive NBA season before being appointed Assistant General Manager in July of 1988.

In college, Suhr was a standout guard and led his Montclair State team to two NCAA College Division tournaments. As a senior, he was named team captain and most valuable player. Also as a senior, he led his team in assists and was second in the nation in free throw percentage.

After graduation, Brendan spent one season as an assistant at the University of Detroit before moving to Fairfield University(CT). At Fairfield he earned his master's degree in educational administration in 1979. Six years in the college

ranks saw his teams compile a 106-57 cumulative record and a birth in the 1978 NIT tournament for Fairfield.

Suhr and his wife, Brenda, have two children, Christina and Brendan Kelly and make their home in the Rochester area. Brendan is one of the NBA's most dedicated distance runners and spends much of his time in the off season with basketball camps and clinics.

Brendan Malone

ASSISTANT COACH

Brendan Malone, a 21-year coaching veteran, begins his second season in 1988-89 as an assistant to head coach Chuck Daly on the Pistons' staff.

Malone replaced Ron Rothstein, who left the Pistons to become the head coach of the expansion Miami Heat. Malone's duties include advance scouting all Pistons' opponents, in addition to his game and practice coaching responsibilities.

Before joining the Pistons, Malone was an assistant coach and scout for the New York Knicks. His duties with the Knicks included scouting college talent and advance scouting NBA opponents in addition to his bench coaching duties.

Malone joined the Knickerbockers in 1986, following a two-year stint as the head coach at the University of Rhode Island.

Prior to coaching at Rhode Island, Brendan was an assistant coach under Jim Boeheim at Syracuse University for six seasons. From 1978 through 1984, the Orangemen posted a record of 134-52 (72 percent), including three NCAA Tournament appearances. Malone was an assistant coach at Fordham University in 1976-77 and at Yale University in 1977-78.

He began his coaching career at Power Memorial Academy in New York City, where he remained for 10 successful

seasons. In Malone's final six seasons at Power Memorial, his teams won a pair of city championships, and he was a three-time New York City "Coach of the Year."

Malone played high school basketball at Rice High School in New York City, and earned his Bachelor's Degree at Iona College in New Rochelle. He earned his master's degree in physical education at New York University. Brendan and his wife Maureen have six children and plan to make their home in metro Detroit.

PISTONS ALL-TIME RECORDS AGAINST NBA OPPONENTS 1957-1989

TEAM	79-80	80-81	81-82	82-83	83-84	84-85	85-86	86-87	87-88	88-89	TOTAL	HOME	ROAD	NEUTRAL
ATL*	0-6	2-4	4-2	3-3	4-2	5-1	2-4	3-3	4-2	5-1	102-130	55-49	36-67	11-14
BOS	0-6	1-4	0-6	3-3	3-3	2-4	1-4	2-3	3-3	3-1	51-153	29-66	17-62	5-25
CHA	—	—	—	—	—	—	—	—	—	4-0	4-0	2-0	2-0	—
CHI	1-1	1-5	6-0	4-2	5-1	3-3	4-2	3-3	4-2	6-0	77-61	48-19	27-40	2-2
CLE	0-6	3-3	5-1	5-1	5-1	5-1	5-1	5-1	5-1	3-3	62-33	35-15	27-18	—
DAL	—	2-0	1-1	0-2	2-0	2-0	2-0	1-1	1-1	2-0	13-5	7-2	6-3	—
DEN	1-1	0-2	1-1	0-2	1-1	2-0	1-1	2-0	1-1	1-1	15-17	9-7	6-10	—
GS#	1-1	0-2	2-0	2-0	1-1	2-0	1-1	1-1	2-0	1-1	77-103	47-32	23-54	7-20
HOU	1-5	1-1	2-0	2-0	1-1	1-1	1-1	1-1	1-1	1-1	45-38	29-10	12-27	4-1
IND	1-5	2-4	2-4	4-2	4-2	6-0	5-1	3-3	3-3	4-2	39-33	27-9	12-24	—
LAC!	0-2	1-1	2-0	1-1	2-0	1-1	2-0	2-0	1-1	2-0	40-20	23-7	17-13	—
LAL%	0-2	0-2	0-2	0-2	1-1	1-1	1-1	1-1	0-2	2-0	72-125	32-52	25-61	15-12
MIA	—	—	—	—	—	—	—	—	—	2-0	2-0	1-0	1-0	—
MIL	1-1	1-5	2-4	3-3	3-2	3-3	2-4	3-3	4-2	2-4	47-74	33-27	14-45	0-2
NJ	2-4	3-3	2-4	3-2	1-4	1-5	4-2	5-1	5-1	4-0	36-32	20-14	16-18	—
NY	2-4	1-5	3-3	1-5	4-2	3-2	4-1	6-0	4-2	0-4	92-115	50-44	30-59	12-12
PHIL+	1-5	1-4	2-3	0-6	3-3	1-5	2-4	5-0	4-1	5-0	76-129	45-44	18-66	13-20
PHOE	0-2	0-2	0-2	1-1	2-0	2-0	0-2	1-1	2-0	2-0	38-38	23-16	14-23	1-0
PORT	0-2	0-2	0-2	1-1	1-1	1-1	1-1	0-2	1-1	1-1	31-30	22-9	10-20	—
SAC$	0-2	1-1	2-0	0-2	1-1	1-1	0-2	1-1	2-0	2-0	102-96	60-21	26-51	16-24
SA	2-4	0-2	0-2	1-1	1-1	1-1	1-1	1-1	1-1	2-0	13-21	6-11	7-10	—
SEA	0-2	0-2	1-1	0-2	1-1	1-1	2-0	2-0	1-1	2-0	40-39	24-14	11-25	5-0
UTAH@	1-1	0-2	1-1	0-2	1-1	0-2	1-1	1-1	2-0	2-0	22-18	14-6	8-12	—
WASH=	2-4	1-5	2-0	3-2	3-3	3-3	4-2	3-3	3-2	5-0	48-29	46-29	23-54	14-9
TOTALS	16-66	21-61	39-43	37-45	49-33	46-36	46-36	52-30	54-28	63-19	1179-1402	687-503	388-759	105-141

*ST.IOUIS1957-68#PHILADELPHIA1957-62,SANFRANCISCO1962-79$CINCINNATI1957-72,KANSASCITY1972-85%MINNEAPOLIS1957-60+SYRACUSE1957-63!BUFFALO1970-78,SANDIEGO1979-84@NEWORLEANS1974-79=CHICAGO1961-63,BALTIMORE1963-74#PHILADELPHIA1957-62,SANFRANCISCO1962-79.

Say what?

1989 - 90 Schedule

Nov.	**3**	**New York (Fri., 8:00)**
	4	@ Washington (Sat., 7:30)
	7	@ Chicago (Tue., 8:00)
	8	@ Indiana (Wed., 7:30)
	10	@ Orlando (Fir., 7:30)
	11	@ Miami (Sat., 7:30)
	15	**Miami (Wed., 7:30)**
	17	**Milwaukee (Fri., 8:00)**
	18	**Boston (Sat., 7:30)**
	21	**Atlanta (Tue., 7:30)**
	24	**Cleveland (Fri., 8:00)**
	26	@ Portland (Sun., 10:00)
	28	@ Sacramento (Tue.; 10:30)
	29	@ Phoenix (Wed., 9:30)
Dec.	1	@ L.A. Lakers (Fri., 10:30)
	2	@ Seattle (Sat., 10:00)
	6	**Washington (Wed., 7:30)**
	8	@ Philadelphia(Fri., 7:30)
	9	**Indiana (Sat., 7:30)**
	12	@ Denver (Tue., 9:30)
	13	@ L.A. Clippers (Wed., 10"30)
	15	@ Utah (Fri., 9:30)
	16	@ Golden State (Sat., 10:30)
	19	**Seattle (Tue., 7:30)**
	22	@ New Jersey (Fri., 7:30)
	23	**Orlando (Sat., 7:30)**
	27	@ Cleveland (Wed., 7:30)
	29	**Milwaukee (Fri., 8:00)**
	30	**New Jersey (Sat., 7:30)**
Jan.	2	@ Orlando (Tue., 7:30)
	3	**L.A. Clilppers (Wed., 7:30)**
	5	**Indiana (Fri., 8:00)**
	6	**New York (Sat. 7:30)**
	9	**Chicago (Tue., 7:30)**
	10	@ Boston (Wed. 7:30)
	12	**Minnesota (Fri., 8:00)**
	13	**Portland (Sat., 7:30)**
	17	@ Philadelphia (Wed., 7:30)
	21	**L.A. Lakers (Sun., 12:00)**
	23	@ Chicago (Tue., 8:30)
	26	**Phoenix (Fri., 8:00)**
	27	@ Minnesota (Sat., 8:00)
	30	@ Atlanta (Tue., 7:30)
	31	**Washington (Wed., 7:30)**

Feb.	3	@ Cleveland (Sat., 1:30)
	4	**Utah (Sun., 1:00)**
	6	**Cleveland (Tue., 8:00)**
	8	@ Milwaukee (Thu., 8:30)
	13	**Denver (Tue., 7:30)**
	17	@ Miami (Sat., 7:30)
	19	**Miami (Mon., 7:30)**
	21	**Orlando (Wed., 7;30)**
	23	@ Atlanta (Fri., 8:00)
	25	@ New York (Sun., 12:00)
	27	**Houston (Tues., 7:30)**
Mar.	1	@ Washington (Thu., 7:30)
	2	**Philadelphia (Fri., 8:00)**
	4	**Indiana (Sun., 7:00)**
	6	**Sacramento (Tue., 7:30)**
	9	@ New Jersey (Fri., 7:30)
	11	@ Charlotte (Sun., 7:00)
	15	**San Antonio (Thu., 7:30)**
	16	@ Chicago (Fri., 8:30)
	18	**Dallas (Sun., 7:00)**
	20	@ Milwaukee (Tues., 8:30)
	22	@ Houston (Thu., 8:30)
	24	@ San Antonio (Sat., 8:30)
	25	@ Dallas (Sun., 8:00)
	28	**Charlotte (Wed., 7:30)**
	30	@ Boston (Fri., 7:30)
Apr.	**3**	**Boston (Tue., 7:30)**
	5	@ Atlanta (Thu., 8:00)
	6	**Milwaukee (Fri., 8:00)**
	8	@ Cleveland (Sun., 12:00)
	10	@ New York (Tue., 8:00)
	11	**New Jersey (Wed., 7:30)**
	13	**Atlanta (Fri., 8:00)**
	14	**Orlando (Sat., 7:30)**
	19	**Philadelphia (Thu., 7:30)**
	20	@ Indiana (Fri., 8:30)
	22	**Chicago (Sun., 1:00)**

All times are Detroit times. **Home games in bold.**